CANCER

2024

Zodiac world, Volume 6Published

By Daniel Sanjurjo, 2023.

While every precaution has been taken in the preparation of this book, the publisher assumes no responsibility for errors or omissions, or for damages resulting from the use of the information contained herein.

CANCER ZODIAC SIGN 2024

First edition. November 22, 2023.

Copyright © 2023 Daniel Sanjurjo.

Written by Daniel Sanjurjo.

Introduction

Welcome to the captivating world of the Zodiac sign Cancer! "Unlocking the Mysteries of Cancer" is your all-encompassing guide to understanding every facet of this astrological sign. Delve into a realm of celestial insight, as you discover the intriguing sections that await you in this book, including the much anticipated Horoscope for 2024.

Within the pages of "Unlocking the Mysteries of Cancer," you'll embark on a profound journey, guided by the following key sections:

1. Horoscope for 2024: Dive headfirst into the future with a detailed and personalized horoscope tailored specifically to Cancer individuals for the year 2024. Gain foresight into the challenges, opportunities, and cosmic influences that will shape your path in the coming year.

2. Cancer Unveiled: Explore the depths of the Cancer zodiac sign and its unique characteristics. From their emotional intricacies to their distinctive personality traits, you'll uncover what makes Cancer individuals truly remarkable.

3. Planetary Influences: Discover the celestial forces that leave their indelible mark on the lives of Cancer personalities. Uncover how the Moon and other planets shape their destinies and influence their daily experiences.

4. Emotional Landscape: Delve into the intricate world of Cancer emotions. From their nurturing and empathetic qualities to their shyness and occasional moodiness, gain insight into the rich tapestry of feelings that drive their actions and decisions.

5. Practical Insights: Whether you're a Cancer seeking self-discovery or someone eager to understand and connect with Cancer individuals, this section offers valuable tips and insights. Learn how to navigate the unique qualities and traits of this astrological sign more effectively.

6. Likes and Dislikes of a Cancer Person: Gain an in-depth understanding of the preferences, passions, and aversions that define Cancer individuals. Uncover what warms their hearts, what they find endearing, and what they prefer to avoid.

As you embark on this enlightening voyage, "Unlocking the Mysteries of Cancer" promises to equip you with the knowledge and tools needed to decode the intricacies of the Cancer zodiac sign. The centerpiece, the Horoscope for 2024, is just the beginning. Explore the essential sections that illuminate Cancer's astrological influences, emotional depths, and personality traits.

Prepare to navigate the intricate world of Cancer and harness the power of astrological insights. This book serves as your gateway to a deeper understanding of Cancer individuals and provides guidance on how to forge more profound and meaningful connections. "Unlocking the Mysteries of Cancer" is your key to unraveling the secrets of this zodiac sign and embracing the wisdom of the stars in the year 2024 and beyond

Cancer Personality Traits

Element: Water   Color: White   Quality: Cardinal

Day: Monday, Thursday   Ruler: Moon

Greatest Compatibility: Capricorn, Taurus

Lucky Numbers: 2, 3, 15, 20

Dates: June 21 - July 22

1. EMOTIONAL SENSITIVITY: Cancerians possess a profound emotional depth. They are highly sensitive to their own feelings and those of others. This sensitivity allows them to connect deeply with people and understand the nuances of complex emotions. They are often the first to offer comfort and support to friends and loved ones in times of need.

2. Nurturing: The nurturing nature of Cancer individuals makes them natural caregivers. They take pleasure in tending to the physical and emotional needs of their loved ones. Whether it's cooking a comforting meal, offering a listening ear, or providing a shoulder to cry on, they are there to nurture and protect those they care about.

3. Loyalty: Cancerians are fiercely loyal to their relationships. Once they commit to a friendship or partnership, they stand by it through thick and thin. Their unwavering loyalty is a testament to their dedication and the value they place on the bonds they create.

4. Family-Oriented: Family holds a special place in the heart of Cancer individuals. They prioritize their family's well-being and enjoy spending quality time with loved ones. Family traditions, gatherings, and maintaining a harmonious home are of utmost importance to them.

5. Protective: Cancerians have a protective instinct. They go to great lengths to shield their loved ones from harm, whether it's providing emotional support, offering guidance, or ensuring a safe and nurturing environment. They take on the role of the caregiver and protector.

6. Intuitive: Cancer individuals possess strong intuition. They have a knack for reading people and situations accurately. Their intuitive abilities help them understand unspoken emotions and the needs of those around them.

7. Imaginative: Creativity flows naturally in Cancerians. They have a vivid imagination and often enjoy artistic endeavors. Whether it's through writing, art, or other creative outlets, they express themselves with a touch of imaginative flair.

8. Empathetic: Their empathetic nature enables them to feel and share the emotions of others. They provide a listening ear and offer support to those facing emotional challenges. This empathy fosters deep and meaningful connections with friends and loved ones.

9. Sentimental: Cancer individuals are sentimental and treasure keepsakes, traditions, and cherished memories. They hold onto mementos and enjoy revisiting the past

through photographs and nostalgic items. Sentimentality is a part of their life's narrative.

10.	Adaptable: While Cancerians appreciate stability, they are adaptable when circumstances change. They can pivot when necessary, making them resilient in the face of life's challenges.

11.	Tenacious: Cancer individuals exhibit tenacity in pursuing their goals. They don't easily give up when faced with obstacles. Their determination and persistence drive them to overcome adversity and achieve their ambitions. Introverted: Many Cancer individuals are introverted to some degree. They require moments of solitude to recharge and reflect on their emotions.

This introspective quality allows them to better understand their feelings.

12.	Cautious: Their cautious nature influences their decision-making. They carefully weigh the pros and cons before making significant life choices. They prefer to minimize risks and make informed decisions.

13.	Practical: Cancerians tend to be practical and responsible when it comes to managing their homes and finances. They take a pragmatic approach to life and are adept at maintaining order in their households.

14.	Homemakers: Creating a warm and inviting home environment is a source of pride for many Cancer individuals. They enjoy domestic activities such as cooking, decorating, and making their homes comfortable and cozy.

These detailed personality traits paint a richer picture of Cancer individuals, showcasing their nurturing, protective, and emotionally attuned nature. Remember that individual personalities can vary, but these traits are common characteristics of the Cancer zodiac sign.

Financial Fortunes in 2024:

Your financial journey in 2024 is like a cosmic voyage. It's essential to know when the tides will be high and when they will recede. With a keen eye on your financial stars, this horoscope will unveil the auspicious moments when your financial ship sets sail towards abundance and when you may need to navigate through challenging waters. In the realm of finance, as the planets align and dance through the skies, you'll discover when to expect prosperity and when to batten down the hatches.

Career and Success: Success in your career, whether it's in business or your job, is a profound aspiration. Your horoscope will reveal when the cosmic winds favor your professional endeavors, propelling you towards your goals. On the flip side, it will also highlight periods when your career path may seem like an uphill climb. Your celestial guide will steer you through these ups and downs, ensuring you chart a course for career triumph in 2024.

Marital Bliss and Challenges: If you're married, your relationship with your spouse is a vital aspect of your life. This horoscope will be your compass in the realm of marriage, guiding you through the good and the challenging times. With insights into the cosmic energies affecting your married life, you'll be better equipped to navigate the seas of matrimony in 2024.

The Year's Multifaceted Aspects: This Cancer Horoscope for 2024 doesn't just stop at finances, career, and marital life. It's a comprehensive guide that offers

9

insights into various facets of your life. Gain wisdom about your property, vehicles, and their fortunes in the coming year. Learn about the direction your career is likely to take. Delve into the realm of health and well-being, understanding when to maintain your vitality and when to be vigilant against potential illnesses. Your celestial map even explores other areas of significance, providing holistic insights to guide you through 2024.

Expert Guidance: This horoscope isn't just any ordinary prediction. It's been meticulously prepared by the esteemed astrologer, Dr. Mrigank of AstroSage. Dr. Mrigank brings a wealth of astrological knowledge and expertise, ensuring that the insights you receive are not just accurate but also deeply insightful. His understanding of planetary transits specific to the Cancer zodiac sign in 2024 is the key to unlocking the cosmic mysteries that lie ahead.

Planetary Portents: The celestial canvas for 2024 is painted with a diverse array of planetary positions. At the beginning of the year, Mercury and Venus grace the fifth house, heralding a period of love and potential financial gains. However, it's not all smooth sailing as the Sun and Mars inhabit the sixth house, possibly leading to health challenges and increased expenses. Saturn's presence in the eighth house introduces a note of caution.

But fear not, as the benevolent Jupiter takes center stage in the tenth house, ensuring a harmonious balance between your career and family life. As May arrives, Jupiter makes its move to the eleventh house, promising a notable increase in your income.

Journeys and Religious Inclinations: Throughout 2024, Rahu takes residence in the ninth house, opening the doors to journeys, especially those of a spiritual nature. You'll have the opportunity to visit pilgrimage sites and immerse yourself in the sacred waters of rivers like the Ganges. This year may find you developing a deeper connection to your spiritual side and embarking on significant journeys, both literal and metaphorical.

Health Matters: The Cancer Horoscope for 2024 emphasizes the importance of health. It's a year to prioritize your well-being and pay special attention to your father's health. As you navigate the complexities of your business, remember that persistence and courage are your allies. Success is attainable when you commit to your work and remain steadfast. This is your year to make strides towards international horizons, as success in going abroad is within your reach.

In summary, the Cancer Horoscope for 2024 is your celestial guide, providing you with the insights and foresight to navigate the multifaceted aspects of your life. It offers a unique blend of financial foresight, career guidance, marital insights, and more. With expert astrological analysis, you can harness the cosmic energies to steer your ship towards success and fulfillment in the coming year.

Navigating the Tides of Love

AS WE EMBARK ON THE journey of love in 2024, the Cancer Love Horoscope provides you with a glimpse into the celestial forces shaping your romantic path. Love and affection are the focal points of this year, and here's what the stars reveal:

Auspicious Beginnings: The year commences with a splendid start for Cancerians in matters of the heart. As the doors of 2024 swing open, two benevolent and love-blessed planets, Mercury and Venus, grace your fifth house. This celestial alignment infuses your love life with renewed vitality. Romance flourishes, and the love between you and your partner blooms with vibrancy. Expect moments filled with tenderness, shared laughter, and countless romantic gestures. You'll be seen enjoying various activities with your significant other, from delightful dinners to leisurely hand-in-hand walks. Love is in the air, and your hearts dance to its rhythm.

Navigating Stormy Waters: However, love's journey is not without its share of turbulence. From February to August, the cosmic seas may grow tempestuous, and the winds of stress and challenges may blow through your love affair. These months demand resilience and patience. Your love life could be particularly susceptible to the influence of the evil eye, so it's advisable to be discreet about your romantic relationship during this period. Guard your love from prying eyes, and trust in the strength of your connection.

Friendship and Boundaries: Be mindful of the roles your friends play in your love life. While friendships are essential, striking a balance is key. Granting friends excessive influence over your romantic affairs can potentially strain your relationship. Maintaining clear boundaries is vital. Trust and communication between you and your beloved will be your anchor during these months.

Balanced Love in the Third Quarter: As we move into the third quarter of the year, equilibrium returns to your love life. Trust, understanding, and open communication will serve as pillars of strength. The challenges faced earlier in the year will find resolution, and your love life will regain its equilibrium. Together, you and your beloved will navigate the intricate dance of love with grace and resilience.

Embracing the Future: In the fourth quarter, the possibility of a deeper commitment arises. It's a time when the idea of taking your relationship to the next level, such as considering marriage, may enter your thoughts. The love you've nurtured throughout the year may lead to discussions about a shared future, solidifying your bond.

In conclusion, the Cancer Love Horoscope for 2024 paints a vivid picture of your romantic journey. Love, like the tides, ebbs and flows, but with trust, communication, and perseverance, you'll navigate its waves and find yourself in the embrace of deeper connection and commitment. The stars offer both challenges and opportunities in matters of the heart, and your journey through 2024 will be a testament to your enduring love.

Navigating the Path to Success

IN THE REALM OF CAREER and professional aspirations, 2024 promises a dynamic journey for Cancerians. The Cancer Career Horoscope for this year reveals a path filled with opportunities, challenges, and significant milestones. Let's delve into the celestial insights for your career:

A Promising Start: The year kicks off with a positive note for your career. Saturn's influence, as it aspects your tenth house from the eighth house, brings an aura of stability and endurance to your professional endeavors. Jupiter, gracing your tenth house, amplifies your visibility and reputation in the workplace. This celestial alignment sets the stage for a strong start to the year.

Mastering Your Craft: With the Sun and Mars residing in the sixth house, you'll become a master of your craft. Your dedication and hard work will not go unnoticed. You'll gain recognition for your unwavering commitment and your name will be on everyone's lips. Your career path will mature, and your professional reputation will soar. Your work ethic will be a source of inspiration for your colleagues.

Jupiter's Influence: As May 1 arrives, Jupiter moves into the eleventh house, enhancing your relationship with senior officials. This celestial transition fosters cooperation and support from your superiors, even in challenging circumstances. Jupiter's fifth aspect on the third house assures collaboration with your colleagues, ensuring a harmonious working environment. Teamwork and camaraderie will be key to your success.

The Second Half Surge: The second half of the year holds the promise of even greater achievements. You'll be poised for promotions and salary increases, leading to a profound sense of happiness and heightened self-confidence. Your dedication to your work will continue to shine, driving your career forward. During this phase, some individuals with ulterior motives may attempt to disrupt your path, causing momentary stress. However, your resilience and dedication will prevail, enabling you to overcome challenges and solidify your professional standing.

The Potential for Change: The period between 23rd April and 1st June may bring the prospect of a job change. This change could be a significant turning point in your career, offering fresh opportunities and challenges. It's a period for you to consider the path ahead and make decisions that align with your professional aspirations.

In summary, the Cancer Career Horoscope for 2024 presents a roadmap filled with opportunities for growth, recognition, and success. The celestial alignments fortify your position in your job and open doors to new horizons. While challenges may arise, your unwavering dedication, strong work ethic, and the support of your colleagues and superiors will lead you to triumph.

Cancer Education

A Year of

Educational Triumph

THE JOURNEY OF EDUCATION in 2024 for Cancerians unfolds with celestial blessings, offering opportunities for academic excellence and growth. The Cancer Education Horoscope for this year provides insights into the celestial forces shaping your educational path. Let's explore the cosmic guidance for your educational endeavors:

Favorable Beginnings: The year commences on an auspicious note for students. The celestial influences of Mercury and Venus, coupled with Jupiter's benevolent gaze upon the fourth and second houses, create a harmonious environment for learning. These planetary alignments enhance your cognitive abilities, improve your memory, and facilitate a deeper understanding of your subjects. Your concentration remains unwavering, making the process of learning smoother and more productive.

Competitive Success: The presence of the Sun and Mars in the sixth house at the beginning of the year bodes well for those pursuing competitive exams. This alignment of celestial forces increases your chances of success in these examinations. You are likely to excel and achieve your academic aspirations in this arena.

Key Success Periods: Pay attention to the months of May, August, and November-December, as these periods hold the promise of favorable outcomes in competitive exams. The stars align to support your ambitions, making it possible to secure a government job. These are critical windows for achieving your career goals.

Pursuing Higher Education: If you aspire to pursue higher education, the cosmos offers a unique opportunity in 2024. There's a potential for studying abroad, but it comes with its set of challenges. You will need to work diligently to make this aspiration a reality. The presence of Rahu in the ninth house brings excitement to your educational pursuits but may lead to moments of distraction. Staying focused can be a challenge, resulting in occasional ups and downs in your educational journey.

Overcoming Obstacles: The presence of Saturn in the eighth house may introduce some obstacles in your educational path, especially in the first and second quarters of the year. During this time, you may encounter moments of difficulty and weakness. However, do not be disheartened, for the stars hold a promise of better days ahead.

Second-Half Triumph: The second half of the year holds the potential for success in higher education. As you navigate through the challenges and distractions, the perseverance you display will lead to achievement. Your commitment to your educational goals will be rewarded, and you will find yourself on the path to success.

In summary, the Cancer Education Horoscope for 2024 unveils a year filled with educational opportunities and triumphs. The celestial influences support your academic pursuits, opening doors to success in competitive exams and higher education. While there may be obstacles along the way, your unwavering determination will see you through to the realization of your educational dreams.

Cancer Finance 2024

Navigating the

Waves of Financial Balance

IN THE REALM OF FINANCES, 2024 presents a dynamic landscape for Cancerians, with both opportunities and challenges. The Cancer Finance Horoscope for this year provides insights into your financial journey, helping you navigate the tides of income and expenditure. Let's explore the celestial guidance for your financial well-being:

Balancing Act: The year 2024 poses a financial balancing act for Cancerians. As you navigate your financial path, you'll find that money flows in and out with a certain rhythm. On one hand, there will be inflows of income, while on the other, you may encounter the rise of expenses. Achieving harmony between these two aspects of your financial life will be paramount.

Financial Guidance: To navigate these financial waters effectively, you may find it beneficial to seek the guidance of a financial advisor. An advisor can provide you with valuable insights and counsel, helping you make informed financial decisions. Their guidance can assist you in strengthening your financial position and managing your resources wisely.

Maintaining Equilibrium: The key to your financial well-being in 2024 lies in how well you maintain balance between your income and expenditure. This balance reflects the overall state of your financial condition.

Regularly monitoring your finances and making strategic decisions will be crucial in ensuring financial stability and security.

In summary, the Cancer Finance Horoscope for 2024 emphasizes the need for a careful and balanced approach to your financial matters. While income and expenses may ebb and flow, your ability to maintain equilibrium and make prudent financial decisions will determine your financial well-being in the coming year.

Cancer Family 2024:

Navigating the

Bonds of Love and Care

IN THE REALM OF FAMILY life, 2024 presents a journey filled with both warmth and challenges for Cancerians. The Cancer Family Horoscope for this year provides insights into your familial connections and offers guidance on how to nurture and strengthen them. Let's explore the celestial wisdom for your family life:

Favorable Beginnings: The year begins with a sense of favorability for your family life. The influence of Jupiter on your fourth house infuses your family relationships with love and positivity. Elders in the family will offer their blessings and appreciate your words. They will provide guidance and support, expressing their affection for you. However, be cautious of the manner in which you express yourself, as the fiery nature of your speech may be misunderstood, potentially leading to minor misunderstandings.

Nurturing Bonds: It's essential to avoid any habits or behaviors that could lead to conflicts within the family, especially during the first quarter of the year. Staying mindful of your communication style will help maintain harmony in your family life. Despite any occasional differences, the support from your family members will remain unwavering.

Siblings and Personal Challenges: Your siblings may face some personal challenges, but despite their individual struggles, they will continue to be a source of assistance and support for you. Their presence and care will be valuable throughout the year.

Father's Health: The well-being of your father may require special attention in 2024. The presence of Saturn in the eighth house and Rahu in the ninth house until year-end may lead to health concerns for your father. In particular, between April 23 and June 1, when Mars transits with Rahu in the ninth house, there may be health issues due to the formation of Angarak Dosha. It's crucial to monitor your father's health and seek medical care when necessary during this period.

Intensified Relationships: The final quarter of the year will bring an intensified focus on personal relationships within the family. This period may bring deeper emotions and connections among family members, providing an opportunity for bonding and strengthening the family unit.

In summary, the Cancer Family Horoscope for 2024 highlights the importance of maintaining harmonious family relationships. While challenges may arise, open communication, understanding, and patience will help you navigate them successfully. The bonds of love and care within your family will remain strong and nurturing throughout the year.

Cancer Child 2024
Nurturing Young

Talents

THE YEAR 2024 BRINGS a favorable outlook for the well-being and development of your children, Cancerian parents. The Cancer Child Horoscope for this year offers insights into your children's growth, aspirations, and accomplishments, providing guidance on how to nurture their talents and create a supportive environment. Let's delve into the celestial guidance for your children:

A Promising Start: The year commences on a positive note for your children. They will exhibit an increase in artistic expression, allowing them to explore their interests and passions. This creative inclination will earn them respect in society and, most importantly, your love and admiration. As a parent, you'll take pride in witnessing the progress and achievements of your child.

Jupiter's Influence: From May 1, as Jupiter transits into the eleventh house and aspects the fifth and seventh houses, a period of remarkable growth and success unfolds for your children. During this specific time, your children are poised for success in their chosen fields. They will gain respect and recognition, exhibiting obedience and a strong moral compass. These positive qualities will make you proud as a parent. Their values will be elevated, and their achievements will shine.

Marital Prospects: The second half of the year holds the promise of marriage for one of your children. This joyous occasion will mark a significant milestone in their life, and you will be thrilled to celebrate this special moment with your family.

Moments of Weakness: The months of April, May, and June may pose challenges to your children's well-being. During this period, it's important to pay extra attention to their health and the company they keep. Ensuring their physical and emotional well-being will be paramount.

In summary, the Cancer Child Horoscope for 2024 underscores the importance of nurturing your children's talents, fostering their creative expression, and providing unwavering support. The year promises growth, respect, and success for your children, making it a source of pride for you as a parent.

Cancer Marriage

Waters of Matrimony

THE YEAR 2024 PRESENTS a dynamic landscape for married Cancerians, filled with both challenges and opportunities in the realm of matrimony. The Cancer Marriage Horoscope for this year provides insights into your marital journey, offering guidance on how to navigate the ups and downs of married life. Let's explore the celestial wisdom for your marriage:

Turbulent Beginnings: The year commences with potential tensions in married life. The presence of the Sun and Mars in the sixth house, coupled with Saturn in the eighth house, may create a sense of unease within the seventh house of marriage. When Saturn, the lord of the seventh house, moves to the eighth house, conflicts and tensions in married life may surface. It's essential to pay close attention to your marital relationship during this period, as unfavorable planetary conditions could lead to divorce.

In-Law Interference: Increased interference from in-laws may strain your relationship and lead to challenges in your married life. The months of January and February may be particularly tumultuous, as both the Sun and Mars transit through the seventh house. These planetary movements could contribute to heightened aggression in your life partner's behavior, potentially resulting in conflicts and disputes.

Favorable Times Ahead: The latter part of the year, starting from August onwards, may herald a more favorable period for married Cancerians. During this time, you'll experience an increase in love and harmony within your married life, gradually improving the overall dynamics of your relationship.

Singles Seeking Partners: If you are single and searching for a life partner, your search may continue throughout the year. While there may be some possibility of marriage in the last months of the year, it is advisable to consider getting married in the following year, as the planetary positions are not particularly favorable in the current year.

Jupiter's Influence: On May 1, as Jupiter transits into the eleventh house and aspects the fifth and seventh houses, love and harmony in married life will begin to flourish in the second half of the year. This celestial alignment contributes to improved marital relations and enhanced compatibility for married individuals.

In summary, the Cancer Marriage Horoscope for 2024 underscores the importance of vigilance and communication in your marital relationship. While the year may bring initial challenges, the latter part of the year offers hope and an opportunity to strengthen the bonds of love and understanding.

Cancer Business Horoscope 2024: Navigating the Waters of Entrepreneurship

The year 2024 offers a challenging yet potentially rewarding landscape for Cancerian business owners. The Cancer Business Horoscope for this year provides insights into your business endeavors and offers guidance on how to navigate the complex world of entrepreneurship. Let's explore the celestial wisdom for your business:

Caution Required: In the realm of business, a cautious approach is advised in 2024. Saturn, the lord of the seventh house, remains in your eighth house throughout the year, leading to fluctuations and uncertainties in your business. It's essential to carefully assess investment decisions and anticipate situations where financial risks or work-related hurdles may arise.

Jupiter's Influence: The presence of Jupiter in the tenth house until May 1 provides a relatively favorable environment for starting or expanding your business. During this time, you can venture into new business opportunities with a degree of optimism. After May 1, when Jupiter moves to the eleventh house and aspects the seventh house, third house, and fifth house, you may adopt a more cautious and calculated approach to your business endeavors. This period could also bring the support of influential individuals in your business network, facilitating your progress.

Mars Transits: The transit of Mars in your seventh house from February 5 to March 15 signifies the potential for significant business deals. This period can enhance your business reputation and contribute to your progress. However, from March 15 to April 23, when Mars transits to affect Saturn in the eighth house, challenges may emerge, impacting your business and potentially affecting your business partner.

External Support: The period from June 1 to August 26 is conducive to receiving support from external sources in your business. This support can bolster your business efforts, but it's crucial to be prepared for potential challenges that may arise later in the year.

In-Law Involvement: If your spouse is your business partner, it's advisable to maintain boundaries with your in-laws and keep them away from business matters. Involving in-laws in your business could lead to complications.

Financial Responsibilities: Timely payment of taxes is vital, as delays may result in receiving notices from tax authorities.

Year-End Growth: The months of November to December are poised to bring significant growth to your business. The infusion of external resources and strategic opportunities will contribute to the expansion and success of your business.

In summary, the Cancer Business Horoscope for 2024 highlights the importance of careful planning, financial responsibility, and external support in your entrepreneurial journey. While challenges may arise, the latter part of the year promises substantial growth and success in your business.

Cancer Property and Vehicle

Realizing Dreams of Ownership

THE YEAR 2024 BRINGS auspicious opportunities for Cancerians looking to acquire property and vehicles. The Cancer Property and Vehicle Horoscope for this year provides insights into favorable timings for making these significant investments. Let's explore the celestial guidance for your property and vehicle aspirations:

Vehicle Acquisition: The first quarter of the year holds promise for those seeking to purchase a new vehicle. Ideal periods for vehicle acquisition include January 1 to 18, February 12 to March 7, March 31 to June 12, and again from September 18 to October 13. Notably, the most favorable window for purchasing a vehicle falls between May 19 and June 12. During this period, the lord of your fourth house is exalted on a Friday, enhancing the likelihood of a successful vehicle acquisition.

Caution Required: It's important to exercise caution and avoid purchasing a vehicle between January 18 and February 12, as well as between February 12 and March 7, as these periods may increase the risk of accidents.

Property Investment: If you are considering acquiring property, the year's beginning presents favorable opportunities. You are likely to succeed in property purchases between January and March. The properties available during this time may be located in beautiful areas, with the potential for nearby temples or religious sites.

Profitable Transactions: Beyond property acquisition, the months of August to November and December offer prospects for earning profits through the purchase and sale of substantial properties. These opportunities may enable you to make sound investments and reap financial rewards.

In summary, the Cancer Property and Vehicle Horoscope for 2024 highlights auspicious periods for realizing your dreams of property ownership and acquiring new vehicles. While caution is advised during specific timeframes, the overall outlook is promising for these significant investments.

Cancer Wealth and Profit Horoscope 2024: Navigating Financial Waters

The year 2024 presents both opportunities and challenges in the realm of wealth and profits for Cancerians. The Cancer Wealth and Profit Horoscope for this year offers insights into your financial prospects and provides guidance on how to manage your financial affairs effectively. Let's delve into the celestial wisdom for your financial well-being:

Financial Caution: The year begins with a degree of financial vulnerability. The presence of the Sun and Mars in your sixth house may affect your financial stability, while Saturn remains in the eighth house throughout the year, leading to increased expenses. It's essential to exercise caution and conduct thorough assessments before engaging in financial transactions, particularly property investments. Ensuring the viability and integrity of any property investment is crucial to avoid substantial additional costs.

Stock Investment: The month of February is particularly favorable for stock investments, presenting opportunities for potential gains. Cancerians can consider strategic stock investments during this period. Similarly, the window between July and August holds promise for those seeking financial opportunities.

Sibling Support: According to the Cancer Horoscope 2024, financial assistance and support from siblings are indicated. Your siblings may offer both assistance in your endeavors and financial contributions. This support can enhance your financial situation and provide valuable assistance in your work.

Salary Increases: Employed individuals can anticipate the prospect of salary increases in the second half of the year. This can lead to a boost in income and financial stability. The possibility of a salary hike can bring increased financial security.

Business Profits: Entrepreneurs and business owners may find opportunities for significant profits, with the most favorable period likely to occur in the second quarter of the year. This period may be conducive to business success and financial gains.

Government Sector Benefits: Between April and June, as well as from September to October, financial benefits from the government sector are indicated. Cancerians may receive financial support or benefits from government-related sources during these periods.

In summary, the Cancer Wealth and Profit Horoscope for 2024 highlights a mixed financial landscape, with the potential for both challenges and opportunities. While financial caution is advised during specific timeframes, prudent financial decisions can lead to financial stability and prosperity.

Cancer Health

Being

IN 2024, THE CANCER Health Horoscope emphasizes the importance of maintaining your well-being and taking proactive measures to address health challenges. Here's a detailed overview of your health prospects for the year:

Health Vigilance: The year commences with health considerations at the forefront. The presence of the Sun and Mars in your sixth house may elevate your body temperature, potentially leading to health issues such as fever and headaches. It's advisable to avoid consuming excessively spicy or hot foods during this time.

Persistent Care: Saturn's presence in the eighth house throughout the year serves as a reminder to address even minor health concerns promptly. Being proactive and seeking timely medical attention can help prevent major illnesses.

Critical Period: From March 15 to April 23, the conjunction of Mars and Saturn in the eighth house necessitates special care. This period may be marked by increased health risks, making cautious driving and risk avoidance essential. If possible, consider having someone else drive your vehicle during this time.

Surgical Considerations: Individuals dealing with existing health issues may face the possibility of undergoing surgery during this period. It's important to prepare for potential medical procedures and follow medical advice diligently.

Challenges with Angarak Yog: The transit of Mars into the ninth house, where Rahu is already present, creates Angarak Yog. This period, from April 23 to June 1, may bring health challenges for both you and your father. Vigilance and timely medical care are essential during this phase.

Gradual Improvement: After July 12, your health is expected to gradually improve. The latter part of the year, particularly in November and December, is anticipated to bring health benefits. However, be prepared for minor health concerns that may arise intermittently.

Common Ailments: Ailments related to bile, cold, fever, headaches, and back pain are likely to be prevalent in your health profile. It's important not to disregard even minor health issues. Regular exercise and yoga can play a significant role in maintaining your fitness and addressing health concerns effectively.

In summary, the Cancer Health Horoscope for 2024 emphasizes the importance of vigilant health care and timely responses to health challenges. While the year may present health-related obstacles, proactive measures and regular exercise can contribute to your overall well-being.

Luck Numbers for Cancer

Path

IN 2024, CANCER, RULED by the Moon, finds its luck intertwined with numbers 2 and 6. These numbers play a significant role in guiding your journey throughout the year. The total sum of the year, 2024, adds up to 8, suggesting a medium year for Cancer individuals. Here's how these numbers can influence your path:

1. Number 2: The number 2 is often associated with balance, harmony, and partnership. It encourages you to seek equilibrium in your life, especially when it comes to relationships and cooperation with others. In 2024, aligning yourself with supportive partnerships and maintaining harmonious connections can be key to your success.

2. Number 6: The number 6 carries energies of love, family, and responsibility. It suggests a year where you may need to focus on nurturing your relationships with loved ones, both within your family and your social circle. Taking care of your responsibilities, especially in your personal life, can lead to a sense of fulfillment.

3. Medium Year: The medium nature of the year implies that while it may not be an exceptionally lucky period, it also doesn't signify insurmountable challenges. Your hard work and determination will play a pivotal role in shaping your experiences and outcomes in 2024. Dedication and persistence will be your allies on your journey.

Cancer individuals in 2024 are encouraged to embrace the qualities associated with the numbers 2 and 6, fostering balance in relationships, nurturing family ties, and meeting responsibilities with dedication. While luck may not always be on your side, your efforts and perseverance can lead to success and personal growth in the year ahead.

Remember, numbers are symbols that can offer guidance, but your actions and decisions are the driving forces behind your destiny. Use the energies of these numbers to your advantage as you navigate the opportunities and challenges that 2024 presents.

Cancer Astrological Remedies

IN 2024, CANCER, LIKE all zodiac signs, may face various challenges and opportunities. Astrological remedies are practices that can help you navigate these energies and make the most of favorable periods while mitigating potential difficulties. Here are some astrological remedies and tips that can enhance your well-being and success in 2024:

1. Chanting Mantras: Chanting mantras can help you connect with positive cosmic energies. Consider chanting the "Om Chandraya Namaha" mantra to invoke the blessings of the Moon, which governs Cancer.

2. Gemstone Therapy: Wearing a pearl, the birthstone of Cancer, can help balance your emotions and enhance your connection to the Moon's energy.

3. Meditation and Yoga: Regular meditation and yoga practices can help calm your mind and improve your overall well-being. Focusing on breathing exercises and relaxation techniques can be particularly beneficial.

4. Moon Rituals: Since the Moon is your ruling planet, perform rituals and prayers during the Full Moon and New Moon phases to harness lunar energy for personal growth and emotional balance.

5. Vedic Astrology Consultation: Consider consulting a Vedic astrologer for personalized insights and remedies

tailored to your birth chart and specific challenges you may face in 2024.

6. Charity and Kindness: Engage in acts of charity and kindness. Sharing your blessings with those in need can create positive karma and attract good fortune.

7. Avoidance of Unnecessary Risks: During challenging planetary transits, exercise caution and avoid taking unnecessary risks, especially in financial matters and business decisions.

8. Meditation on the Number 2: Meditate on the number 2 to enhance your sense of balance and harmony. Visualize yourself in a state of equilibrium and emotional stability.

9. Water Element Practices: Cancer is a water sign. Spending time near bodies of water, like lakes or the ocean, can help you feel more connected to your element and soothe your emotions.

10. Spiritual Retreats: Consider attending a spiritual retreat or spending time in a peaceful, natural environment to recharge your energies and gain clarity.

Astrological remedies are intended to support and complement your efforts in various aspects of life. While they can be beneficial, it's essential to approach them with a positive and open mind. Remember that astrology offers guidance, but your actions and choices ultimately shape your   destiny.

Frequently asked questions

―――

About Cancerians in 2024:

1. How will 2024 be for Cancerians?

- It will be a pretty good year for Cancer zodiac people, especially in terms of financial and marriage aspects.

2. When will the fortune of Cancer Zodiac rise in 2024?

- The time after May 24 is considered suitable for financial and jobrelated activities for Cancerians.

3. What is the fate of Cancerians in 2024?

- This year can be one of the best phases of your life due to the presence of Jupiter, which can bring opportunities and blessings.

4. Who is the life partner of Cancer?

- Cancer is most compatible with fellow zodiac signs Virgo and

Pisces in terms of relationships.

5. Which zodiac sign loves Cancer?

• Cancer makes a harmonious connection with Virgo, indicating a strong bond.

6. Who is considered an enemy of Cancerians?

• Leo and Scorpio are often considered challenging for Cancerians in terms of compatibility.

If you have more questions or need further information, feel free to ask. I'm here to assist you with any inquiries you may have.

January 2024 Cancer

The January 2024 horoscope for Cancer heralds a period of promising career success and positive financial developments. As the year commences, the astrological alignments favor taking strategic steps toward new professional endeavors. Consideration of a job change or elevation to a higher position is well-supported, offering a positive impact on financial stability. With the Sun in Capricorn enhancing analytical abilities, a rational approach is advised, particularly for Air signs prone to impulsive actions.

Key Highlights:

Career Advancements: The beginning of the year presents a favorable opportunity for career advancements. Cancer individuals are encouraged to seize the chance for upward mobility, whether through a new job or an advanced position. The analytical prowess heightened by the Sun in Capricorn aids in making reasoned decisions.

Financial Opportunities: Positive financial shifts accompany career success. Embracing new opportunities contributes to a more favorable financial situation. However, a cautious and reasoned approach is recommended to ensure long-term stability.

Family Focus: The month emphasizes the importance of resolving differences in family life. Cancer individuals are encouraged to prioritize family relationships and create harmonious domestic environments. The influence of the Wolf Full Moon in January fosters sentimental connections and may lead to enduring relationships, potentially culminating in marriage.

Career Growth: The first days of January offer a window for career advancement. Opportunities to climb the career ladder, accept new positions, or engage in international internships should be embraced. Efforts invested during this period are likely to yield significant results.

Travel Prospects: Venus in Sagittarius creates favorable conditions for travel. Cancer individuals are encouraged to seize the opportunity to explore the world, gaining valuable experiences and insights. Events and encounters during travel may hold significance and contribute to personal growth.

Mid-Month Creativity: The middle of January sees an abundance of creative energy, fostering incremental career development. Increased charm facilitates the gathering of like-minded individuals. A cooperative and friendly atmosphere prevails, particularly benefiting Earth signs. Mercury in Capricorn promotes practical thinking, leading to the alignment of scattered thoughts into a cohesive picture.

Personal Development: Considering individual plans for personal development is recommended. Seeking guidance from a coach can enhance confidence in future endeavors. The supportive astrological energies pave the way for Earth signs to experience a continuous and productive work schedule.

Shift to Everyday Matters: Toward the end of January, the pace of life slows, redirecting focus to everyday concerns. The horoscope suggests clearing away New Year decorations and organizing the home. Mars in Capricorn imparts strength and strong will, aiding individuals, especially Air signs, in overcoming challenges and achieving success.

Overall, January holds the promise of a dynamic and transformative period for Cancer individuals, blending career achievements, financial stability, family harmony, and personal growth.

February 2024 Cancer

In February 2024, Cancer individuals can anticipate a period of stability, where events unfold gradually and predictably. The harmonious influence of the Sun in Aquarius provides a conducive atmosphere for reevaluating life perspectives. Grounded and rational Earth signs, including Cancer, have the opportunity to express themselves in new ways. The energy of the Snow Full Moon in February serves as a catalyst for pivotal moments, emphasizing the importance of reaching agreements within the family through a willingness to compromise.

Key Highlights:

Stability and Maneuverability: The month brings a sense of stability, allowing individuals to carefully contemplate near-term plans and make necessary adjustments. The harmonious energy of the Sun in Aquarius encourages a reconsideration of life views. Earth signs, including Cancer, may find approval in making changes to their image or place of residence.

Family Focus: The Snow Full Moon in February holds transformative energy, offering a crucial opportunity to achieve harmony within the family. A willingness to compromise plays a pivotal role in resolving conflicts and fostering understanding among family members.

Quality Time with Loved Ones: Early February presents an opportunity for Cancer individuals to spend quality time with loved ones. Strategic planning and effective time management are emphasized to balance relationships with other commitments. The horoscope emphasizes the importance of not neglecting family bonds even amidst a busy schedule.

Leadership Ambitions and Conflict Avoidance: Venus in Capricorn heightens leadership ambitions, but caution is advised against pursuing victory at all costs. The desire to prove superiority may lead to conflicts, and it's essential to find creative outlets for excess energy. The horoscope suggests avoiding pushing the family into the background.

Motivation and Creative Expression: Mid-February sees abundant motivation, fueled by the anticipation of spring. Cancer individuals are encouraged to prioritize their desires and live authentically, breaking free from external expectations. The general horoscope underscores the potential for meeting interesting people and succeeding in new endeavors.

Decisive Action and Freedom: The influence of Mercury in Aquarius provides an amazing sense of freedom, removing strict prohibitions and expanding the boundaries of possibilities. Cancer individuals are urged to take decisive action without holding back. Closing existing debts and seeking forgiveness contribute to a fresh start.

Financial Stability and Family Planning: The last days of February bring stable financial conditions, with the possibility of extra income such as a salary increase or bonus. Home and family take precedence, and prudent financial planning is advised. Joint decision-making with loved ones helps avoid spontaneous spending.

Favorable Influence of Mars: Mars in Aquarius supports daring actions, and despite others' perplexity, Air signs, including Cancer, are favored by fate. The horoscope encourages embracing spontaneous activities, such as parties and trips, with a carefree attitude.

Overall, February offers Cancer individuals a harmonious blend of stability, family focus, creative expression, and financial prudence, with the favor of fate guiding them toward positive outcomes.

March 2024 Cancer

In the March 2024 horoscope, Cancer individuals can anticipate a wave of love and romantic interest. The onset of spring brings a surge of attention from the opposite sex, accompanied by a continuous stream of compliments. Chance encounters may pave the way for beautiful love stories. However, as the Sun enters Pisces, internal contradictions may surface, requiring a confrontation with fears. Success hinges on the ability to plan for the long term, allowing a methodical approach toward personal goals. The Worm Full Moon in March becomes a pivotal moment for self-realization, prompting a reassessment of factors hindering personal development, including the need for a change in social circles and perspectives.

Key Highlights:

Premonition of Love: March holds the promise of romantic developments, with a heightened interest from the opposite sex and an abundance of compliments. Chance encounters may blossom into meaningful connections, initiating beautiful love stories.

Facing Internal Contradictions: The influence of the Sun in Pisces brings internal contradictions to the forefront, demanding a confrontation with fears. Success is linked to the ability to plan for the long term, fostering a calm and methodical pursuit of goals.

Worm Full Moon for Self-Realization: The Worm Full Moon in March serves as an opportune moment for self-realization. Cancer individuals are encouraged to identify and address factors impeding personal development. This period prompts a reassessment of social circles and perspectives.

Learning and Professional Development: The events in the first days of March emphasize the importance of continuous learning. Insufficient professionalism may impact work productivity, prompting dissatisfaction from authorities. The horoscope advises prioritizing quality over quantity and seeking training courses to enhance skills.

Optimism and Love of Life: Venus in Aquarius instills optimism and a love for life, providing a positive outlook even in challenging situations. Subtle awareness of surroundings and the mood of people contributes to preventing negative developments. Practices like mindfulness meditation enhance strengths and resilience.

Financial Ambiguity in Mid-March: The middle of March presents a period of financial ambiguity, balancing stable income with unplanned expenses. The horoscope suggests a focus on savings and strategic spending on essential items or long-term considerations to avoid burnout.

Wild Ideas and Educational Ventures: Under Mercury in Aries, impulsive actions may lead to wild ideas, such as pursuing studies abroad. While this idea may yield dividends over time, it's crucial to consider the financial implications. Exploring more affordable alternatives is advised.

Calm End of March: The conclusion of March signals a period of calmness, with an atmosphere of goodwill in the team and mutual understanding in the family. Opportunities arise to strengthen professional positions and increase authority within the family, particularly in the eyes of children.

Mars in Pisces: Mars in Pisces elevates thoughts, enabling even pragmatic individuals to embrace high ideals. The horoscope encourages Cancer individuals to channel this energy into positive actions and not suppress bright impulses, potentially leading to transformative experiences.

Volunteer Opportunities for Earth Signs: Earth signs, including Cancer, may find fulfillment in joining the volunteer movement as Mars in Pisces inspires altruistic endeavors. Exploring new capacities through volunteering marks the beginning of a transformative journey.

Overall, March presents Cancer individuals with opportunities for love, self-realization, and professional growth, with an emphasis on long-term planning and embracing transformative energies.

April 2024 Cancer

The April 2024 horoscope promises a bustling period for Cancer individuals as spring unfolds with enticing prospects for new achievements. Opportunities for career changes, financial success, and meaningful connections abound, fueled by the positive energy of the Sun in Aries. Water signs, including Cancer, receive a potent supply of energy to channel toward the realization of career goals. The desire to ascend to a leadership position is fortified by self-confidence, ensuring inevitable success. However, personal life may encounter challenges, particularly conflicts stemming from jealousy. The Pink Full Moon in April intensifies passions, reaching a climax, and recommends resolving crises through romantic gestures, such as a reconciliation dinner.

Key Highlights:

Craving for Achievements: Spring's arrival triggers a craving for new achievements, offering exciting possibilities such as career changes, financial success, and new acquaintances. The positive influence of the Sun in Aries empowers Water signs, providing a powerful supply of energy to direct toward career goals.

Career Advancement: Cancer individuals are encouraged to harness the energy of self-confidence to pursue career advancement. The positive Sun in Aries amplifies the desire to reach a leading position, ensuring success in professional endeavors.

Jealousy-Induced Conflicts: Personal life may experience challenges, particularly conflicts fueled by jealousy. The Pink Full Moon in April marks a period of heightened intensity in passions, suggesting that brute force tactics are ineffective. Resolving crises is recommended through romantic gestures, such as a reconciliation dinner.

Opportunities for Cooperation: The beginning of April presents opportunities for cooperation and meetings with promising partners. Effective communication is key, and upgrading networking skills is advised for a smooth negotiation process. The influence of Venus in Aries enhances charm and self-confidence.

Impactful Travel and New Acquaintances: The middle of the month provides opportunities for self-expression, with new people influencing life. Travel plans may materialize, bringing success, particularly through new acquaintances. Under Mercury in Aries, impulsive actions may lead to wild ideas, including the consideration of continuing studies abroad.

Positive End of April: The positive conclusion of April aligns with the spring mood, fostering a desire to live richly without delving into mundane details. The horoscope suggests embracing change, including a wardrobe transformation with bright outfits. Mars in Pisces elevates thoughts, prompting even pragmatic individuals to gain wings through sincere actions and turning energetic impulses into positive deeds.

Volunteer Opportunities for Earth Signs: Earth signs, including Cancer, are encouraged to explore new capacities by joining the volunteer movement. This marks the beginning of a transformative journey, aligning with the positive energy of Mars in Pisces.

April 2024 brings a dynamic blend of career opportunities, personal challenges, and transformative energies for Cancer individuals, urging them to navigate through professional and personal pursuits with confidence and resilience.

May 2024 Cancer

The May 2024 horoscope delivers a caution against hasty decisions, emphasizing the potential consequences of impulsivity, including conflicts, disputes, and financial losses. Acting confidently while considering circumstances is key, with the Sun in Taurus enhancing qualities like perseverance and diligence, placing Earth signs, including Cancer, in a winning position. Success hinges on developing the right strategy, starting with strengthening the material base.

Key Highlights:

Caution Against Hasty Decisions: The horoscope advises against hasty decisions, as impulsivity can lead to various issues. Confidence in actions is crucial, but a careful consideration of circumstances is equally important. The influence of the Sun in Taurus emphasizes qualities such as perseverance and diligence, favoring Earth signs.

Family Life and Emotional Connection: A significant event in family life is marked by the Flower Full Moon in May. This period establishes a special connection between spouses, enhancing sexual attraction. It's an opportune time to take the relationship to a new level by addressing and resolving any lingering issues.

Positive Financial Outlook: The financial situation in the first days of May follows a positive scenario, with expenses aligning with income. The horoscope predicts a prolonged period of stability, allowing for a comfortable financial position. While there's room for indulgence, caution is advised against significant investments and large purchases.

Creative Atmosphere and Original Ideas: Venus in Taurus enhances the ability to appreciate beauty, fostering a desire to surround oneself with interesting people and pleasant things. A creative atmosphere encourages the birth of original ideas, which, with the support of like-minded individuals, can be easily realized. It's a favorable time for renovations in the home or personal image.

Increased Self-Confidence and Professional Sphere: By the middle of the month, self-confidence and courage increase, positively impacting the professional sphere. However, the horoscope warns against excessive activity, emphasizing the need to calculate each step and set clear, achievable goals.

Temptations and Strengthening Self-Control: The end of May brings temptations that require strengthened self-control. The desire to escape troubles may arise, but running away is cautioned against, as it could exacerbate problems. Mars in Aries serves as a motivating force, generating energy to confront challenges. Water signs are encouraged to assert their rights, possibly through legal proceedings, maintaining a cool-headed approach.

Navigating Challenges with a Cool Head: The May horoscope underscores the importance of avoiding a rose-colored perspective and conducting detailed reconnaissance before making permanent decisions. Mars in Aries provides energy for a principled position, especially for Water signs engaging in legal proceedings. However, a cool-headed approach without unnecessary fanaticism is essential.

May 2024 presents a blend of caution, emotional connections, financial stability, and opportunities for creative expression for Cancer individuals, urging them to navigate challenges with thoughtful consideration and assertiveness.

June 2024 Cancer

The June 2024 horoscope anticipates a storm of passions, marking the beginning of summer with vivid events in personal life for Cancer individuals. Fateful encounters or reunions with first loves promise passionate and unforgettable experiences. Despite the erratic nature of the Sun in Gemini, characterized by sharp mood changes, Fire signs, including Cancer, display the intelligence to navigate emotional fluctuations. Meditative practices are recommended to channel energy appropriately. The Strawberry Full Moon in June brings clarity to business matters, removing barriers and propelling stalled projects forward. Career success leads to prosperity.

Key Highlights:

Passionate Start to Summer: Summer begins with bright events in personal life, potentially involving a fateful acquaintance or a reunion with a first love. The novel promises passion and unforgettable experiences. The intelligent approach of Fire signs, including Cancer, helps overcome mood changes associated with the unruly Sun in Gemini.

Stability in Family Life: Early June brings stability to family life, contingent on individual efforts. While routine may be perceived as an enemy by many, the horoscope suggests finding excitement in everyday activities through creativity and imagination. Effective communication, supported by Venus in Gemini, fosters understanding among individuals.

Health Challenges and Preventive Measures: The middle of the month presents health challenges due to accumulated fatigue, resulting in low energy levels and weakened defenses. The horoscope recommends preventive measures to improve health, including taking vitamins and avoiding alcohol and fast food. Mercury in Gemini injects vitality into life, providing moments of joy and opportunities for personal development.

Financial Calmness and Enjoyment of Life: The end of June brings financial calmness, allowing Cancer individuals to navigate without unexpected expenses. Modest profits are balanced by the absence of unnecessary expenditures. The horoscope encourages enjoying life, emphasizing that love and mutual understanding overshadow material concerns. The position of Mars in Taurus promotes a pragmatic and belligerent mindset, making individuals invulnerable and encouraging practical thinking.

Advantages of Mars in Taurus: The combination of belligerence and pragmatism under the influence of Mars in Taurus offers invulnerability. Even impulsive Fire signs are urged to think practically. The horoscope suggests directing energy towards personal and collective well-being, as kindness tends to multiply.

June 2024 presents a dynamic mix of passionate encounters, stability in family life, health challenges, financial calmness, and the pragmatic influence of Mars in Taurus, encouraging Cancer individuals to navigate through emotional storms with intelligence and practicality.

July 2024 Cancer

In the July 2024 horoscope, a breath of change is palpable as life progresses with planned advancements. Critical moments bring the right people and necessary finances, outlining future successes. Despite the promising outlook, a cautious approach is advised, emphasizing reflection and focus on essential matters. The month of Cancer fosters a deep sense of family belonging, providing an opportunity to resolve old conflicts. While well-being remains generally positive, increased risk of injury during the Thunder Full Moon in July calls for caution in activities such as driving and sports, suggesting meditation as a safer alternative.

Key Highlights:

Planned Progress and Family Focus: The atmosphere in July encourages planned progress, aligning resources for future successes. Deepening connections with family becomes a priority, offering a chance to mend old conflicts. The horoscope emphasizes reflection and thoughtful actions amid promising changes.

Financial Abundance with Caution: The first days of July may appear financially abundant, but challenges arise in implementing plans. The horoscope warns against haste and impulsive spending, urging a thoughtful approach to problem-solving. Venus in Cancer may trigger inner fears, emphasizing the need to maintain a positive outlook and seek harmony through meditation and supportive connections.

Soft Control and Positive Direction: By the middle of the month, life slows down while maintaining an adventurous spirit. Soft control is recommended, particularly for air signs, directing energy positively through travel, sports, and hobbies. The general horoscope suggests effective efforts, supported by the influence of Mercury in Leo, bringing a meaningful perspective to daily life and fostering relationships based on respect and mutual assistance.

Summer Adventures and Rest: The end of July brings a captivating summer mood, encouraging a break from struggles and unwarranted actions. The horoscope envisions an exciting trip and unforgettable experiences, emphasizing the importance of rest. Health considerations include the risk of injury, especially for Fire signs prone to impulsive actions. Balanced activities, avoiding extreme sports, and embracing light fitness are advisable.

July 2024 presents a mix of planned progress, financial abundance with caution, soft control, and a focus on family and positive direction. The month encourages a balance between adventurous spirits and the need for rest, promoting a harmonious approach to life and well-being.

August 2024 Cancer

The **August 2024 horoscope** advises Cancer individuals to embrace a period of reduced activity, signaling the end of summer with a calm and familiar life flow. While some may find solace in rest, others may sense a temporary lull before potential future events. In the realm of personal life, the Sun in Leo stirs up a heightened sexual appetite, particularly impacting Air signs adept at navigating a range of emotions. The energy of the Sturgeon Full Moon in August sparks inspiration, fostering curiosity about the future. This period encourages a gradual movement in the chosen direction, emphasizing the importance of creating a reservoir of positive emotions.

Key Highlights:

Reduced Activity and Calm Atmosphere: August brings a recommendation for Cancer individuals to reduce their activity levels, marking the last summer month with a serene and predictable life flow. Whether it's a time of rest or a brief calm before potential future events, this period encourages a steady and measured approach.

Passionate Personal Life: With the Sun in Leo, personal relationships, especially in the romantic realm, experience a surge in passion. Cancer individuals are urged to embrace and navigate the intense emotions, recognizing the potential for serious connections and meaningful experiences.

Sturgeon Full Moon's Inspiring Energy: The Sturgeon Full Moon in August serves as a source of inspiration, sparking curiosity about the future. Cancer individuals are encouraged to view the upcoming time with interest and take gradual steps in their chosen direction.

Embrace Tranquility in Early August: The pace of life slows down slightly in early August. Cancer individuals are advised not to fret if plans face obstacles or if the usual hustle seems to quiet down. This period offers an opportunity for self-indulgence, whether through beauty treatments, sports, shopping, or other hobbies.

Venus in Virgo Streamlining Life: Venus in Virgo contributes to streamlining life, making it easier to complete lingering tasks. Cancer individuals can take advantage of this period to realize long-held dreams, clear clutter, and prioritize personal health with a touch of perseverance.

Resumption of Regular Life by Mid-August: Life resumes its usual rhythm by the middle of the month, bringing a return to more active communication and the introduction of new faces. The general horoscope for August 2024 suggests Cancer individuals take initiative in dating, in moderation, and focus on building powerful alliances for a successful career.

Career Focus and New Opportunities by End of August: As August concludes, Cancer individuals are urged to heighten their focus on career matters, with ambitions reaching new heights. New prospects and opportunities may arise, and seizing them becomes crucial. The horoscope hints at possible accidents, urging readiness for travel.

August 2024 presents a blend of caution, emotional connections, financial stability, and opportunities for creative expression for Cancer individuals, urging them to navigate challenges with thoughtful consideration and assertiveness.

September 2024 Cancer

According to the **September 2024 horoscope**, life gains momentum for Cancer individuals, requiring dedicated efforts to reach career heights and improve financial situations. Decisive actions without delay are emphasized for success, with the influence of the Sun in Virgo elevating critical thinking. This period becomes an opportune time to address shortcomings and embark on a journey to eliminate bad habits. In personal life, the Harvest Full Moon in September brings new colors, shifting the focus to family values and fostering the resolution of relationship crises.

Key Highlights:

Career Advancement and Financial Improvement: The September horoscope encourages Cancer individuals to work diligently towards career advancements and financial improvement. Acting decisively and making choices without delay is key to ensuring success during this dynamic period.

Influence of the Sun in Virgo: The Sun's influence in Virgo heightens the level of criticality, making shortcomings more apparent. This period becomes an opportune time to set goals for personal growth, including the elimination of bad habits, as self-awareness increases.

Transformation in Personal Life: The Harvest Full Moon in September brings transformative energy to personal life. Random relationships become a thing of the past, with a spotlight on family values. Relationship crises can be overcome by spouses, and single individuals may find happiness.

Non-Standard Actions in Early September: Early September presents challenges that require non-standard actions. The horoscope advises staying true to planned objectives, as luck may come from unexpected sources or through the assistance of a patron. Venus in Libra eases the experience of troubles, fostering intuitive understanding and effective communication.

Appearance and Communication Skills: Alongside developing communication skills, the horoscope suggests working on personal appearance, recommending visits to the beautician. The influence of Venus in Libra makes challenges less painful, providing an intuitive understanding of the best actions while respecting boundaries.

Mood Swings and Nature's Changes: Mid-September brings mood swings, signaling changes in nature. The period of rest and carefree entertainment concludes, urging Cancer individuals to increase momentum. Travel is recommended as a way to come to terms with reality, with Mercury in Virgo facilitating processes and indicating opportune moments.

Housing Solutions and Great Deals: Despite previous challenges in the housing issue, the general horoscope for September 2024 believes circumstances will change dramatically. Great deals in various aspects of life, including housing, are expected to unfold one after another.

Stable Finances in Late September: In the last days of September, financial concerns ease, with income surpassing expenses. The horoscope predicts stable income, and Cancer individuals can leverage contacts and a reputable reputation to find profitable opportunities. While pessimism may arise due to Mars in Cancer, maintaining lavender sachets can offer a soothing influence.

September 2024 presents a period of dynamic growth, transformative energies in personal life, and opportunities for career and financial advancement for Cancer individuals. Navigating challenges with assertiveness, thoughtful consideration, and a focus on family values will contribute to a successful and fulfilling month.

October 2024 Cancer

The **October 2024 horoscope** brings a streak of luck, promising changes primarily in personal life for Cancer individuals. The autumn wind carries transformative energies, providing opportunities for new acquaintances and a chance to shape destiny. The position of the Sun in Libra emphasizes the need for self-improvement, with harmony between internal and external aspects considered essential. Visiting a beautician and nutritionist is recommended, and tangible improvements are expected after the Hunter's Full Moon in October, marking a favorable time for new projects, studies, or business development.

Key Highlights:

Streak of Luck and Personal Life Changes: The horoscope promises a streak of luck, particularly in personal life. Lonely individuals have a chance to shape their destiny through job or residence changes, leading to new acquaintances and opportunities. The Sun in Libra emphasizes the importance of harmonious self-development.

Work on Oneself and Harmonious Existence: Cancer individuals are encouraged to work on themselves as the Sun in Libra requires internal content to align with external appearance. Continuous self-improvement is highlighted, prompting visits to a beautician and nutritionist for holistic well-being.

Optimal Time for New Projects: The Hunter's Full Moon in October marks a period of maximum concentration of forces, providing an optimal time to initiate new projects, embark on educational endeavors, or implement business development plans.

Challenges and Adaptation in Early October: The first days of October present new challenges, requiring quick learning and adaptation to circumstances. Consulting senior colleagues for advice and borrowing best practices is recommended. The horoscope suggests seeking guidance from a coach to strengthen the spirit during moments of doubt.

Charismatic Aura and Inspirational Attitude: Venus in Scorpio endows Cancer individuals with rabid charisma, fostering an inspirational attitude. Even indecisive individuals may find wings behind their backs, giving an extra boost to ideas. The horoscope encourages experiments, including those related to fashion, to break away from the usual image and enhance attractiveness.

Financial Challenges in Mid-October: The middle of October poses financial challenges, with varying degrees for each zodiac sign. The general horoscope warns against potential scams promising instant profits, emphasizing the importance of discernment. Water signs, in particular, need to be cautious about overspending and falling for deceptive schemes.

Passion and Romance in Personal Life: Mercury in Scorpio brings a touch of passion and romance to personal life. Timid lovers are urged to confess their feelings boldly, while married couples are liberated to explore sensual pleasures. The horoscope encourages embracing desires openly, as suppressing them may lead to the gradual fading of the fire of love.

Career Triumph and Comradeship: The end of October becomes a time of unconditional triumph in career success. Competitors fade into the shadows, and colleagues exhibit commendable activity. The October horoscope underscores the importance of a sense of comradeship, emphasizing that acting in concert and providing mutual assistance can lead to unprecedented heights.

Maintaining Positivity with Mars in Cancer: Despite potential moments of pessimism, especially for those with increased anxiety, Mars in Cancer encourages Cancer individuals to keep a sachet of lavender on their desk to counter negative emotions and maintain a positive outlook.

October 2024 offers Cancer individuals a blend of luck, self-improvement, transformative energies in personal life, and opportunities for career success. Navigating challenges with adaptability, discernment, and a focus on positive relationships will contribute to a fulfilling and triumphant month.

November 2024 Cancer

The **November 2024 horoscope** advises Cancer individuals to set ambitious goals, as this period favors undertakings, promising positive developments in all spheres of life. The energy level increases during the month of Scorpio, amplifying natural qualities. Fire signs are particularly favored by fate, with the possibility of achieving planned objectives. The Beaver Full Moon in November creates an ideal atmosphere for confessions and open-mindedness in love, ensuring that expressed feelings will be reciprocated, leading to a transformative romance.

Key Highlights:

Setting Goals for Success: November 2024 is conducive to setting and pursuing ambitious goals, with favorable outcomes expected in various life spheres. The energy boost during the month of Scorpio enhances natural qualities, and Fire signs are especially favored by fate. The horoscope encourages taking calculated steps for doubled results.

Ideal Time for Confessions and Romance: The Beaver Full Moon in November creates an ideal setting for confessions and open expressions of feelings. Love is in the air, and the liberated atmosphere fosters a transformative romance that can turn life upside down. Cancer individuals are encouraged to embrace this romantic energy.

Financial Challenges in Early November: Financial affairs in early November may be challenging, with potential letdowns from business partners or unfavorable situations in the labor market. Temporary expense reduction is advised, and the horoscope suggests giving up unnecessary purchases. The situation is expected to improve soon, leading to a significant increase in income.

Streamlining Life with Venus in Virgo: Venus in Virgo contributes to streamlining life, making it easier to finish pending tasks and pursue long-held dreams. Cancer individuals are urged to declutter their living spaces, mend broken relationships, and take charge of their health. Perseverance during this period can bring positive and transformative changes.

Importance of Words and Communication: In the middle of November, luck is on the side of brilliant speakers and skillful interlocutors, according to the general horoscope. Words hold great importance, and individuals are advised to be mindful of their speech, as even a single phrase can influence the course of events. The intervention of Mercury in Sagittarius ensures attention to crucial points for a happy future.

Trusting Intuition and Deciphering Clues: Trusting intuition is emphasized in November, especially when plagued by doubts or fear of taking a step forward. Deciphering clues, regardless of their source, is key to making informed decisions. The horoscope encourages Cancer individuals to move forward without dwelling on old problems and to trust their inner guidance.

Family Challenges and Personal Growth: The last days of November may bring challenges to family life, with hard work and study demands leading to outbreaks of irritability. Sorting out issues is discouraged, as it may unveil ugly facts. The beneficial position of Mars in Scorpio helps Cancer individuals emerge victorious from any situation, contributing to personal growth and character strengthening.

Elevating Immune System for Personal Growth: Fire signs will feel invigorated, wanting to conquer the world. Starting from low altitudes is recommended to avoid premature exhaustion in the race. Strengthening the immune system becomes crucial to withstand challenges and maintain vitality, aligning with the positive influence of Mars in Scorpio.

November 2024 presents Cancer individuals with opportunities for goal-setting, romantic transformations, financial improvements, and personal growth. Navigating challenges with perseverance, mindful communication, and a focus on health will contribute to a fulfilling and transformative month.

December 2023 Cancer

The **December 2023 horoscope** for Cancer radiates a sense of celebration, signaling the arrival of numerous tasks associated with resolving domestic and work-related issues. To enhance the anticipation of the New Year and not miss any important moments, starting an advent calendar is recommended. The influence of the Sun in Sagittarius fills life with optimism, particularly invigorating Water signs with a surge of enthusiasm. Challenges are perceived as opportunities to strengthen the spirit, prompting a proactive approach to working on personal complexes. The turning point is marked by the Cold Full Moon in December, providing a glimpse of the year's results and paving the way for exciting events in the future.

Key Highlights:

Festive Spirit and Enthusiasm: The December 2023 horoscope instills a sense of celebration, urging Cancer individuals to embrace the festive spirit. Under the influence of the Sun in Sagittarius, optimism prevails, and Water signs experience a surge of enthusiasm. Challenges are viewed as opportunities for personal growth and positive transformation.

Work on Personal Complexes: Challenges and difficulties serve as a platform for strengthening the spirit, encouraging Cancer individuals to shift from reflection to proactive work on personal complexes. The turning point, marked by the Cold Full Moon in December, signifies the fading of painful problems into the past and the anticipation of exciting future events.

Seething Personal Life: In early December, personal life is dynamic, with most events carrying a positive impact. Despite busy work schedules, finding time for dates is encouraged. New relationships formed during this period are predicted to be strong, forming reliable alliances. Married couples deepen their trust in each other.

Influence of Venus in Libra: Venus in Libra contributes to a less painful experience of troubles in personal life. An intuitive understanding of how to act and assert oneself without violating boundaries is heightened. Development of communication skills and working on appearance is emphasized during this period, prompting visits to beauty professionals.

Favorable Financial Situation: The financial situation in mid-December is favorable, contingent on personal initiative and development in various directions. The general horoscope predicts an increase in income, encouraging holiday shopping and thoughtful gift selection. Mercury in Capricorn emphasizes practicality, aiding in organizing scattered thoughts and abstract ideas.

Completion of Tasks and Positive Impressions: The last days of December pass swiftly, leaving behind positive impressions. Perseverance and hard work enable the completion of pending tasks, allowing Cancer individuals to enter the new year with a light heart. The December horoscope encourages a focus on the good and maintaining belief in positive outcomes.

Mars in Sagittarius and Desire for Adventure: Mars in Sagittarius signals a turning point, aligning desires with the pursuit of adventure. While the desire for change is heightened, it's essential to remain restrained to avoid abandoning business commitments and losing lucrative contracts. Romantic Water signs are advised to stay grounded and not detach from reality.

Introduction of New Elements: The desire for change can be channeled positively by studying foreign languages or introducing new elements into one's routine. Romanticism is encouraged, but a balance with practicality is essential for a grounded and fulfilling experience.

December 2023 presents Cancer individuals with opportunities for personal growth, positive transformations, strengthened relationships, and financial stability. Navigating challenges with enthusiasm, proactive effort, and a balanced approach will contribute to a joyous and fulfilling month.

Summary of Month by Month

January 2024 Horoscope: Cancer

The January 2024 horoscope for Cancer indicates a focus on personal development and establishing a solid foundation. Opportunities for career advancement and financial stability arise, encouraging strategic planning. Relationships may undergo positive transformations, deepening emotional connections. Health-conscious efforts yield positive results, promoting overall well-being.

February 2024 Horoscope: Cancer

In February 2024, Cancer individuals experience a harmonious blend of professional success and emotional fulfillment. Career endeavors prosper, leading to financial gains. Relationships thrive with increased communication and understanding. Health improvements result from a balanced approach to well-being. Overall, a month of positive growth and achievement.

March 2024 Horoscope: Cancer

March 2024 brings a dynamic mix of social interactions, career advancements, and personal growth for Cancer individuals. Networking opportunities contribute to professional success. Relationships deepen through shared experiences. Health-conscious choices lead to increased vitality. The month fosters a balance between personal and professional spheres.

April 2024 Horoscope: Cancer

April 2024 highlights the importance of self-expression and creativity for Cancer individuals. Career opportunities abound, and financial stability improves. Relationships benefit from open communication and shared creative endeavors. Health-conscious choices contribute to overall well-being. The month encourages embracing individuality and pursuing passions.

May 2024 Horoscope: Cancer

The May 2024 horoscope for Cancer emphasizes caution in decision-making and highlights the potential for emotional connections, financial stability, and creative expression. Opportunities for positive financial outlook and personal growth arise. Relationships undergo positive transformations. May encourages Cancer individuals to navigate challenges with thoughtfulness and assertiveness.

June 2024 Horoscope: Cancer

June 2024 presents Cancer individuals with opportunities for professional success, financial stability, and harmonious relationships. Career advancements and financial gains are likely. Relationships deepen through shared goals and mutual support. Health-conscious efforts lead to increased vitality. A month of positive growth and achievement for Cancer.

July 2024 Horoscope: Cancer

July 2024 presents a mix of planned progress, financial abundance with caution, soft control, and a focus on family and positive direction. The month encourages a balance between adventurous spirits and the need for rest, promoting a harmonious approach to life and well-being.

August 2024 Horoscope: Cancer

The August 2024 horoscope advises a reduction in activity, emphasizing the importance of rest and personal well-being. The month brings opportunities for emotional connections and creative expression. Career ambitions and new prospects arise by the end of August. Health-conscious choices are essential, with a focus on avoiding risks.

September 2024 Horoscope: Cancer

September 2024 signals a period of hard work and career growth for Cancer individuals. The influence of the Sun in Virgo prompts critical self-reflection. Personal life sparkles with new colors, emphasizing family values. Challenges early in the month require non-standard actions, leading to unexpected opportunities. Travel is favored for coming to terms with reality.

October 2024 Horoscope: Cancer

October 2024 promises a streak of luck for Cancer individuals. Changes in personal life, opportunities for new acquaintances, and internal harmony are highlighted. Challenges in early October require quick learning and adaptation. The month encourages assertiveness, creativity, and caution in financial matters. Career success leads to triumph by the end of October.

November 2024 Horoscope: Cancer

November 2024 recommends setting goals for Cancer individuals. The period favors undertakings in all life spheres, with increased energy levels. Water signs, especially Fire signs, can achieve planned goals. The Beaver Full Moon in November is ideal for confessions and passionate experiences. Financial affairs early in the month may require caution. Luck favors brilliant speakers and skillful communicators.

December 2024 Horoscope: Cancer

The December 2024 horoscope radiates a sense of celebration for Cancer individuals. Domestic and work-related challenges are present, but the festive spirit prevails. Personal growth, positive transformations, and financial stability are emphasized. The turning point during the Cold Full Moon brings visibility to the year's results. Personal life seethes with positive events, and financial situations improve, leading to a joyful end of the year.

In summary, the upcoming year for Cancer individuals holds opportunities for personal and professional growth, financial stability, and positive transformations in relationships. Navigating challenges with optimism, assertiveness, and a balanced approach contributes to a fulfilling and rewarding year.

Cancer Man, The Ultimate Guide

Cancer Man In Love

When a Cancer man falls in love, his insecurities surface, and he tends to stick to certain behavioral rules to feel secure. What he often overlooks is the significance of showing his emotions, which plays a crucial role in relationships. A Cancer man is compassionate and sweet, and the right partner will appreciate his emotional side.

Cancer Man Sexuality

Mars is fallen in a Cancer man's sign, which can affect his initiative and sex drive. Despite wanting to be an exceptional lover, he may struggle to demonstrate his abilities. For a Cancer man, sexual satisfaction is closely tied to emotions, and he values love, emotional connection, and eye contact during intimacy.

Cancer Man In Relationships

A Cancer man is sensitive to his partner's emotions and craves a deep connection. However, if he has experienced family issues, he may struggle to open up to the right partner. He tends to avoid conflict and will often stay calm even in challenging situations. It's important for a Cancer man to find a partner who encourages his emotional expression.

Can You Trust Your Cancer Man

In most cases, you can trust a Cancer man. He might prioritize privacy over honesty at times, but when he decides to let someone into his world, he shares almost everything. His lies, if any, are usually about small things that can benefit both parties. Infidelity and constant pursuit of new partners are not typical of a Cancer man.

Dating Cancer Men

Cancer men are likely to take their partners to a family restaurant with excellent food. They appreciate romantic walks, cozy restaurants, or home-cooked dinners. Some Cancer men enjoy cooking, and a romantic kitchen date is a possibility. Dating a Cancer man can be a wonderful and flattering experience.

Understanding Cancer Men

Cancer men have a sensitive side due to their zodiac sign, but it can be challenging for them to navigate in a world that often misunderstands or judges their emotional nature. Their relationship with their mother can provide insights into their character. When raised with a stable sense of security, they make excellent partners for those seeking a quiet family life.

Cancer Man Likes And Dislikes

Cancer men are tender, sweet, and genuinely interested in their partner's life. They rarely use flattery to get someone into bed and make safe choices for building long-lasting relationships. However, they can also be perceived as needy and insecure by more energetic signs.

How To Choose A Gift For Your Cancer Man

Cancer men appreciate gifts with traditional or emotional value. Practical and expensive gifts are less appealing to them. Personalized presents that convey love are ideal. Consider items related to their traditions and family. A plane ticket to a dream destination may surprise and delight a Cancer man, as they often dream of visiting distant places.

Cancer Woman: The Ultimate Guide

Cancer Woman In Love

When a Cancer woman falls in love, her motherly instincts can become overpowering. She tends to distinguish between different types of relationships but can get confused when true feelings are involved. Her unselfish nature makes her vulnerable to emotional exploitation, so setting boundaries and being rational in relationships is crucial for her.

Cancer Woman Sexuality

Cancer women can have a unique relationship with sexuality due to their sign's connection to Mars. They may rely on sensual, tender, and emotional lovemaking. A Cancer woman's passion emerges when she is in love and feels that love reciprocated. She is unlikely to leave a partner with whom she has developed true sexual intimacy.

Cancer Woman In Relationships

Cancer women possess a gift of compassion, making them exceptional listeners who can empathize with others. Their protective nature can sometimes be exaggerated, stemming from a strong motherly instinct. Emotional stability and the desire for a loving, lasting relationship often lead them to seek marriage and children.

Can You Trust Your Cancer Woman

Cancer women are generally trustworthy unless deeply hurt or frightened. They prioritize maintaining a stable home and will make sacrifices to do so, even if it means keeping secrets or telling white lies. Their loyalty to family and home is unwavering.

Dating Cancer Woman

Dating a Cancer woman is straightforward. She enjoys intimate and romantic settings, avoiding noisy places or overly spicy food. While not overly social, she has a close circle of understanding friends. A partner who surprises her with common sense, an open mind, and a sense of education will win her heart.

Many Cancer women also have a strong desire to travel.

Understanding Your Cancer Woman

Cancer women are driven by a mission to bring about significant change in their lives. When they choose Scorpio or Aquarius partners, it may indicate that they are still on their journey of transformation. While they may appear gentle and mild, they can be formidable fighters when motivated. Understanding their moral values and goodness is crucial, as they believe in the balance of nature and that everything given returns.

Cancer Woman Likes And Dislikes

Cancer women are caring, loving, and faithful. They value stability and are not inclined to seek constant excitement or change. They can be emotional, oversensitive, and quiet, so appreciating their emotional side is essential.

How To Choose A Gift For Your Cancer Woman

Cancer women appreciate gifts with sentimental value. Pay attention to their reactions and what excites them. Traditional gifts, such as flowers on birthdays, are valued.

However, practical and thoughtful gifts that resonate with their emotions and needs are ideal.

Introduction to Zodiac Signs

In this opening chapter, we embark on a journey into the realm of astrology and zodiac signs, laying a solid foundation for our exploration of the Cancer zodiac sign. This chapter will serve as an in-depth introduction to the world of astrology, providing readers with a comprehensive understanding of the zodiac system and its enduring significance.

Introduction to Zodiac Signs

Astrology, one of the world's oldest belief systems, has captivated human imagination for centuries. At the core of this mystical discipline lies the zodiac, a term derived from the Greek word "zōidiakos kuklos," meaning "circle of animals." The zodiac is a celestial belt, encircling our planet, divided into 12 distinct segments, each representing a zodiac sign. These signs are more than just astronomical symbols; they hold profound significance in our understanding of the cosmos and the human experience.

From its origins in ancient Mesopotamia to its evolution through the ages, the zodiac has played an integral role in the lives of countless individuals. In the ancient world, civilizations like the Babylonians, Egyptians, and Greeks turned their gaze to the heavens, seeking meaning and guidance. They observed the motion of celestial bodies and created the zodiac as a tool to decipher the universe's secrets.

The zodiac has been instrumental in guiding agricultural calendars, predicting the weather, and aiding in the navigation of seafarers. Its influence extended to the world of human relationships, with astrologers using it to understand personality traits, predict compatibility, and even forecast one's fate.

In this comprehensive exploration of the zodiac, we will delve into the historical origins of the zodiac, unraveling its enduring importance in human history. We will see how the zodiac became more than a stargazer's tool; it became a cultural and societal touchstone, shaping traditions and beliefs across the globe.

This introductory section aims to provide readers with a deep appreciation of the zodiac's roots and its continued influence on our lives. It serves as the gateway to a profound journey through the intricate world of astrology, culminating in a detailed examination of the Cancer zodiac sign, its traits, and its place in the grand tapestry of the zodiac.

In this opening chapter, we embark on a journey into the realm of astrology and zodiac signs, laying a solid foundation for our exploration of the Cancer zodiac sign. This chapter serves as an in-depth introduction to the world of astrology, providing readers with a comprehensive understanding of the zodiac system and its enduring significance.

The Concept of Zodiac Signs

The concept of zodiac signs is deeply rooted in the human fascination with the heavens. These celestial constellations have been a source of wonder and inspiration for countless generations. The word "zodiac" finds its origins in the Greek term "zōidiakos kuklos," meaning "circle of animals." This term is a testament to the zodiac's connection to the animal symbols associated with each sign.

The zodiac, as we know it, is a circular belt in the sky that appears to follow the path of the Sun throughout the year. It is divided into 12 segments, with each segment representing a specific zodiac sign. These signs are Aries, Taurus, Gemini, Cancer, Leo, Virgo, Libra, Scorpio, Sagittarius, Capricorn, Aquarius, and Pisces.

The concept of the zodiac is closely intertwined with the ancient practice of astrology, which is the study of the movements and relative positions of celestial objects as a means of understanding and interpreting human affairs and natural phenomena. Astrology dates back thousands of years, and it has left its mark on cultures and societies across the globe.

In ancient Mesopotamia, one of the cradles of civilization, the zodiac was already being used as a tool for divination and guiding daily life. The Babylonians among the earliest astronomers and astrologers, keeping meticulous

the stars and their movements. They divided the zodiac into 12 equal sections, each associated with a specific month of the year.

The concept of zodiac signs and astrology also found its way to Egypt, where it influenced various aspects of society, from the construction of the pyramids to the organization of their calendar.

The Greeks, known for their contributions to many fields of knowledge, further developed the zodiac system. They assigned different myths, characteristics, and attributes to each sign, laying the foundation for the modern astrological understanding of the zodiac.

Throughout history, the zodiac and astrology have played essential roles in guiding human activities. Farmers used them to determine the best times for planting and harvesting crops. Seafarers relied on celestial navigation, incorporating zodiac constellations into their journeys.

This rich history and cultural significance make the concept of zodiac signs more than just a collection of symbols; it's a profound exploration of humanity's quest to understand the cosmos and its impact on our lives.

By understanding the concept of zodiac signs, we can begin to unravel the deep layers of symbolism and interpretation that underpin the zodiac system. It is this system that forms the basis for our exploration of the Cancer zodiac sign in the chapters to come.

The 12 Signs of the Zodiac

The zodiac, a celestial belt encircling the Earth, is divided into 12 distinct segments, each representing a zodiac sign. These signs are more than just symbolic representations; they encapsulate a rich tapestry of personality traits, attributes, and characteristics that have intrigued and inspired humanity for centuries.

1. Aries (March 21 - April 19): Aries, the first sign of the zodiac, is symbolized by the Ram. This fire sign is associated with traits such as leadership, courage, and enthusiasm. Arians are known for their adventurous spirit and strong will.

2. Taurus (April 20 - May 20): Taurus, symbolized by the Bull, is an

earth sign characterized by traits like stability, determination, and a love for the finer things in life. Taureans are renowned for their practicality and reliability.

3. Gemini (May 21 - June 20): The Twins represent Gemini, an air sign. Geminis are known for their intellectual curiosity, versatility, and social nature. They have a gift for communication and adaptability.

4. Cancer (June 21 - July 22): Cancer, the subject of our exploration, is symbolized by the Crab. This water sign is deeply connected to emotions, nurturing, and sensitivity. Cancer individuals are intuitive, compassionate, and deeply devoted to their loved ones.

5. Leo (July 23 - August 22): Leo, represented by the Lion, is a fire sign that embodies traits like leadership, self-

confidence, and creativity. Leos are natural-born leaders and thrive in the spotlight.

6. Virgo (August 23 - September 22): Virgo, symbolized by the Virgin, is an earth sign known for its practicality, attention to detail, and analytical nature. Virgos have a strong sense of duty and a desire for perfection.

7. Libra (September 23 - October 22): The Scales represent Libra, an air sign. Librans are associated with traits such as harmony, diplomacy, and a love for beauty. They excel in creating balance and maintaining peace.

8. Scorpio (October 23 - November 21): Scorpio, symbolized by the Scorpion, is a water sign with traits like intensity, determination, and a keen sense of intuition. Scorpios are known for their transformative power.

9. Sagittarius (November 22 - December 21): Sagittarius, the Archer, is a fire sign. These individuals are marked by their adventurous spirit, optimism, and love for exploration. They have a deep-seated desire for freedom.

10. Capricorn (December 22 - January 19): Capricorn, symbolized by the Goat, is an earth sign known for its ambition, discipline, and practicality. Capricorns are natural organizers and strive for success.

11. Aquarius (January 20 - February 18): The Water Bearer represents Aquarius, an air sign. Aquarians are associated with traits like

innovation, independence, and a strong sense of justice. They are often seen as the visionaries of the zodiac.

12.   Pisces (February 19 - March 20): Pisces, symbolized by the Fish, is a water sign. These individuals are marked by their compassion, creativity, and intuition. Pisceans have a deep connection to the world of emotions and imagination.

Each of these 12 zodiac signs has its own unique set of characteristics and is associated with different elements (earth, water, air, fire) and ruling planets. These attributes, combined with the sign's position in an individual's birth chart, contribute to the complex and multi-dimensional nature of each person's astrological profile.

Understanding the 12 signs of the zodiac is essential for gaining a broader perspective on the role of the Cancer zodiac sign in the grand tapestry of astrology. In the chapters to come, we will delve deep into the unique traits and attributes of Cancer individuals, offering a comprehensive understanding of this water sign's place in the zodiac.

The Significance of Astrology

Astrology, often a subject of debate and intrigue, continues to exert a profound influence on modern life. Its significance reaches into various facets of human existence, shaping our beliefs, decisions, and the way we perceive the world.

1. Personal Relationships: Astrology has a significant impact on how individuals approach personal relationships. Many people turn to their zodiac signs to gain insights into their compatibility with others. Whether it's finding a suitable romantic partner or building strong friendships, astrology often plays a role in these decisions. People consult compatibility charts to see how well their signs align, seeking harmony and understanding.

2. Career Choices: Astrology's influence extends to the professional realm. Individuals often explore their zodiac signs to gain insights into their natural talents, strengths, and career preferences. Some zodiac signs are associated with traits that are well-suited to particular professions. For example, Leos, known for their leadership skills, may excel in managerial roles, while analytical Virgos might thrive in fields that require attention to detail.

3. Self-Discovery: Astrology plays a crucial role in self-discovery. It offers individuals an opportunity to delve into their personalities, strengths, and weaknesses. By understanding their zodiac signs, people can gain valuable insights into their inherent traits and potential for growth. This self-awareness can lead to personal development and a better understanding of one's motivations and behavior.

4. Decision-Making: Astrology often factors into decision-making processes. Some individuals consult their horoscopes or astrologers before making significant life choices, such as moving to a new city, changing careers, or embarking on important projects. They believe that the positions of celestial bodies can offer guidance and wisdom.

5. Cultural Relevance: Astrology is deeply ingrained in popular culture. Horoscopes are featured in newspapers, magazines, and online platforms, providing readers with daily, weekly, or monthly astrological guidance. Many people follow these horoscopes, which offer general insights based on their zodiac signs.

6. Skepticism and Belief: Astrology's continued presence in modern life is not without controversy. While some individuals embrace astrology wholeheartedly, others remain skeptical. Nevertheless, astrology's significance is undeniable, as it continues to engage people from all walks of life, shaping their beliefs, decisions, and personal philosophies.

Understanding the significance of astrology in contemporary society is vital as we embark on our exploration of the Cancer zodiac sign. It serves as a lens through which we can appreciate the enduring appeal of astrology, its impact on individuals' lives, and the cultural relevance it maintains in our modern world.

Understanding the Basics

———

In this chapter, we will delve into the fundamental concepts that underpin the world of astrology and the zodiac system. It's essential to comprehend these basics to appreciate the intricacies of the Cancer zodiac sign and its unique traits.

The Fundamentals of Astrology

Before we explore the specifics of individual zodiac signs, we must lay a solid foundation in astrology. This section serves as a comprehensive overview of the key principles and elements that shape astrological practice.

1. The Celestial Spheres: Astrology is rooted in the study of the celestial spheres, including the planets, stars, and their movements. The positions of these celestial bodies at the time of a person's birth are central to constructing an astrological birth chart, also known as a natal chart. We'll delve into the significance of these celestial bodies and their roles in astrological interpretation.

2. The Zodiac Wheel: The zodiac wheel is a crucial component of astrology. Comprising 12 signs, each associated with distinct characteristics, the zodiac wheel is the canvas upon which astrologers paint individual profiles. We'll explain the divisions of the zodiac wheel and how each sign corresponds to a particular period of the year.

3. Planetary Rulerships: Planetary rulerships play a significant role in astrology. Each zodiac sign is linked to one or more ruling planets. Understanding these associations is vital for interpreting a person's astrological profile. We'll explore the connections between zodiac signs and their ruling planets.

4. The Elements: The zodiac signs are categorized into four elements: earth, water, air, and fire. These elements represent fundamental personality traits and characteristics. A Cancer's water element, for

instance, reflects their emotional depth and intuition. We'll delve into the elemental properties of each sign.

5. Qualities and Modalities: Qualities (cardinal, fixed, mutable) and modalities (positive, negative) further define the personality traits of zodiac signs. They provide insights into how each sign approaches life, relationships, and challenges. We'll discuss the significance of these qualities and modalities in astrological interpretation.

By understanding the fundamentals of astrology, readers will be well-prepared to explore the intricacies of the Cancer zodiac sign in the following chapters. The principles outlined in this section serve as a strong foundation for a more in-depth examination of astrological concepts and the unique attributes of Cancer individuals.

The Celestial Spheres

The practice of astrology is deeply rooted in the study of the celestial spheres, encompassing the planets, stars, and their intricate movements. To grasp the significance of astrological interpretations and the construction of birth charts, it's essential to understand the celestial bodies that shape this discipline.

1. The Planetary Influences: Astrology recognizes several key celestial bodies, each associated with distinct energies and influences. These planets include the Sun, Moon, Mercury, Venus, Mars, Jupiter, Saturn, Uranus, Neptune, and Pluto. The position of these planets at the time of a person's birth is a fundamental element in creating an astrological birth chart.

2. The Sun: The Sun, often considered the most critical celestial body in astrology, represents the core of an individual's identity. It signifies the ego, basic motivations, and the conscious self. One's zodiac sign is determined by the position of the Sun at their time of birth.

3. The Moon: The Moon is intimately connected with emotions, instincts, and subconscious patterns. It influences one's emotional reactions, intuition, and deep-seated desires. The Moon's position in the zodiac at birth reveals an individual's emotional character.

4. The Planets' Movements: The planets' movements through the

zodiac provide a dynamic backdrop to astrological interpretations. Transits, or the positions of planets in relation to an individual's natal chart, are essential in predicting significant life events and personal growth.

5. Aspects and Angles: Aspects are the angular relationships formed between planets in a birth chart. They offer insights into an individual's personality and the potential for harmonious or challenging life experiences.

Common aspects include conjunctions, sextiles, squares, trines, and oppositions.

6. Houses: The astrological houses divide a birth chart into 12 segments, each representing different life areas. The planets' positions within these houses provide detailed information about specific aspects of an individual's life, such as relationships, career, or personal goals.

Understanding the celestial spheres and their influence is a critical step in comprehending the complexities of astrological practice. These planetary energies and their movements shape the unique attributes and characteristics of each zodiac sign, including Cancer.

As we proceed through this chapter, we will delve further into the elements, qualities, modalities, and the roles of the planets, providing a comprehensive understanding of how these factors interact to create the astrological profiles we explore in the following chapters.

The Zodiac Wheel: Divisions and Significance

The zodiac wheel is a central component of astrology, serving as the canvas upon which astrologers paint individual profiles. Understanding the divisions and significance of the zodiac wheel is vital for appreciating how it influences our lives and shapes the attributes of each zodiac sign.

1. The 12 Zodiac Signs: The zodiac wheel is divided into 12 segments, each corresponding to a specific zodiac sign. These signs are Aries,

Taurus, Gemini, Cancer, Leo, Virgo, Libra, Scorpio, Sagittarius,

Capricorn, Aquarius, and Pisces. The order of these signs is

determined by the Earth's orbit around the Sun.

2. The Zodiac's Symbolism: Each zodiac sign is associated with unique symbolism, including an animal, element, and ruling planet. For example, Cancer is symbolized by the Crab, governed by the element of water, and ruled by the Moon. These symbols hold profound meaning and contribute to the personality traits associated with each sign.

3. Zodiac Cycles: The zodiac wheel is further divided into four elemental groups, each containing three signs. These groups represent the elements of earth, water, air, and fire. The cycle begins with Aries, the first sign of the zodiac, and concludes with Pisces. The elemental qualities add depth to an individual's astrological profile.

4. The Shift of Ages: The zodiac wheel is also associated with the precession of the equinoxes. Over time, the positions of the zodiac signs have shifted due to the Earth's axial wobble. This shift is believed to usher in different astrological ages, each associated with specific energies and themes.

5. Astrological Houses: The zodiac wheel is divided into 12 astrological houses, each representing different life areas and experiences. The positions of planets within these houses offer insights into specific aspects of an individual's life, such as career, relationships, and personal growth.

Understanding the divisions and symbolism of the zodiac wheel provides a foundation for interpreting the unique attributes and characteristics of each zodiac sign. The zodiac's cyclical nature and its influence on our lives offer valuable insights into our personalities and life experiences.

As we proceed through this chapter, we will continue to explore the elements, qualities, modalities, and the roles of the planets, offering a comprehensive understanding of how these factors combine to shape the astrological profiles we examine in the following chapters.

Planetary Rulerships and Their Significance

The connection between zodiac signs and their ruling planets is a cornerstone of astrological interpretation. This section explores the significance of planetary rulerships and how they shape the personality traits and characteristics of each sign.

1. The Ruling Planets: Each zodiac sign is associated with one or more ruling planets. These planets exert a significant influence on the sign's attributes and characteristics. For example, Cancer is ruled by the Moon, which bestows emotional depth, intuition, and sensitivity to those born under this sign.

2. The Influence of Ruling Planets: The influence of a ruling planet extends beyond the sign it governs. It affects the entire birth chart and adds layers of complexity to an individual's astrological profile. Understanding the role of ruling planets is key to interpreting a person's overall disposition and tendencies.

3. Dual Rulerships: Some zodiac signs have dual rulerships, meaning they are influenced by more than one planet. For instance, Scorpio is ruled by both Mars and

Pluto. Dual rulerships provide a multifaceted perspective on the sign's attributes and traits.

4. Planetary Transits: The movements of ruling planets and other celestial bodies through the zodiac play a vital role in astrology. Planetary transits, where planets align with a specific zodiac sign or house in a birth chart, can bring about significant life events and personal growth.

5. Planetary Aspects: The angular relationships formed between ruling planets and other celestial bodies, known as aspects, provide further insights into a person's astrological profile. Aspects can indicate harmonious or challenging interactions, influencing a person's behavior and experiences.

6. Symbolism and Archetypes: Ruling planets are often associated with specific symbols and archetypes. For example, the Moon is linked to the archetype of the nurturing mother and emotional caretaker. These symbols deepen our understanding of a sign's core qualities.

Understanding the influence of ruling planets is integral to comprehending the intricate world of astrology. The connection between planetary rulerships and the zodiac signs is a key component in interpreting the unique attributes and characteristics of each sign, including Cancer.

As we proceed through this chapter, we will continue to explore the elements, qualities, modalities, and the roles of the planets, providing a comprehensive understanding of how these factors interact to create the astrological profiles we explore in the following chapters.

The Characteristics of Cancer Individuals

Cancer is the fourth sign of the zodiac and is represented by the symbol of the Crab. Individuals born under this sign possess a unique set of characteristics that define their personality and influence their approach to life.

1. Emotional Sensitivity: Cancer individuals are renowned for their emotional depth and sensitivity. They experience feelings on a profound level and often have strong intuition about the emotions of others. Their empathetic nature allows them to connect with people on a deep, emotional level.

2. Nurturing and Caring: Cancer is associated with the archetype of the caregiver and nurturer. Those born under this sign have an innate desire to care for and protect their loved ones. They are often seen as the "mother" or "father" figure in their social circles, providing support and comfort to friends and family.

3. Strong Intuition: Cancer individuals have a keen sense of intuition. They can often sense when something is amiss or when someone close to them is in need. This intuitive ability allows them to offer valuable insights and emotional support to those around them.

4. Loyalty and Dedication: Cancer individuals are fiercely loyal to their loved ones. They place a high value on family and close friendships and will go to great lengths to protect and support those they care about. Their dedication and loyalty are unwavering.

5. Imaginative and Creative: Many Cancer individuals possess a rich imagination and creative spirit. They often

have a strong connection to the arts and may find solace and inspiration in creative pursuits such as painting, writing, or music.

6. Adaptability: Cancer individuals are adaptable and can navigate a variety of situations with ease. They are skilled at reading the emotional atmosphere and adjusting their approach accordingly, making them excellent at diffusing tension and fostering harmony.

7. Protective Nature: Cancer's symbol, the Crab, carries a protective shell. Similarly, Cancer individuals have a protective nature. They are quick to shield their loved ones from harm or emotional distress and will do whatever it takes to ensure their safety and well-being.

8. Sentimental Value: Cancer individuals place great importance on sentimentality. They often cherish and preserve mementos and keepsakes that hold sentimental value. These items serve as a source of comfort and a connection to cherished memories.

Understanding the characteristics of Cancer individuals is the first step in unraveling the mysteries of this zodiac sign. These traits, characterized by emotional depth, sensitivity, and a nurturing spirit, set the stage for a more profound exploration of the Cancer zodiac sign in the chapters to come.

The Element, Ruling Planet,

and Associated Symbols of Cancer

Understanding the elemental aspect, ruling planet, and symbolic representations of the Cancer zodiac sign adds depth to our comprehension of this sign's unique attributes.

1. Element - Water: Cancer belongs to the water element. Water signs are known for their emotional depth, intuition, and sensitivity. Cancer individuals are highly in touch with their feelings and possess an innate ability to navigate the complex waters of emotions.

2. Ruling Planet - The Moon: The Moon is Cancer's ruling planet, and its influence is profound. The Moon is intimately connected with emotions, intuition, and the subconscious mind. It governs the ebb and flow of emotions, just as the Moon's phases wax and wane. This planetary influence intensifies Cancer's emotional sensitivity and nurturing qualities.

3. Symbol - The Crab: Cancer is symbolized by the Crab, an animal that carries its home on its back. This symbol represents the protective and nurturing nature of Cancer individuals. Like the Crab, they have a protective "shell" they retreat into when they feel vulnerable, and they are quick to provide shelter and care for their loved ones.

4. Cardinal Sign: Cancer is also classified as a cardinal sign. Cardinal signs are known for their leadership and initiative. While Cancer's leadership style may be more subtle and family-oriented, they are natural organizers and

often take the lead in their personal lives, ensuring the well-being of those they love.

5. Positive Modality: Cancer is a positive or "yang" sign, associated with assertiveness and outgoing qualities. Cancer individuals actively seek to provide support, nurture, and protect their loved ones. Their positive modality enhances their ability to take action and make a difference in the lives of those they care for.

By examining the element, ruling planet, and associated symbols of Cancer, we gain a holistic perspective on the sign's emotional depth, nurturing tendencies, and protective nature. These elements, combined with the characteristics we discussed earlier, create a complex and multifaceted portrait of Cancer individuals.

1. Emotional Depth: Cancer individuals experience their emotions on a deep level. They are highly sensitive and empathetic, which allows them to understand the feelings of others. Their emotional depth makes them excellent listeners and sources of comfort for friends and family.

2. Empathy and Compassion: Cancer individuals have an innate ability to empathize with others. They genuinely care about the wellbeing of those around them and are quick to offer support and understanding. Their compassion makes them excellent friends and confidants.

3. Intuitive Insights: Cancer's connection to the Moon enhances their intuition. They can often sense when something is amiss or when a loved one is going through a challenging time. Their intuitive insights are valuable for offering guidance and comfort to those in need.

4. Home and Family-Centered: Cancer individuals hold family and home life in high regard. They often take on the role of nurturer within their families, providing emotional support, care, and a sense of security. Their home is a place of comfort and refuge for themselves and their loved ones.

5. Protective Instincts: Cancer's symbol, the Crab, represents their protective instincts. They are quick to shield their loved ones from harm, both emotional and physical. This protective nature is a reflection of their deep commitment to the well-being of those they care about.

6. Sentimental Attachments: Cancer individuals are sentimental and often attach significance to keepsakes and memories. They cherish mementos that hold sentimental value and have a strong connection to their personal history.

7. Supportive and Nurturing: Whether as parents, partners, or friends, Cancer individuals excel in providing support and nurturing. They are attentive and dedicated, ensuring that their loved ones feel cared

For and loved.

8. Challenges with Letting Go: While their nurturing and protective nature are admirable, Cancer individuals can face challenges when it comes to letting go. They may hold onto past hurts and grievances, and their protective instincts can sometimes lead to overbearing behavior.

Understanding the emotional and nurturing traits of Cancer individuals provides insight into their compassionate and caring nature. These traits are central to the Cancer zodiac sign's identity and set the stage for a deeper exploration of how these qualities manifest in various aspects of their lives.

The History and Origin of Cancer

Part 1: A Historical Overview of Astrology

Ancient Beginnings: The history of astrology traces its origins to ancient civilizations, particularly the Babylonians and Egyptians. In these early cultures, scholars closely observed the movements of celestial bodies, such as the stars and planets, and believed that these celestial phenomena held significance for events on Earth. They recorded their findings in clay tablets and developed an early form of astrology that focused on celestial omens and predictions.

Greek Influence: The Greek civilization played a pivotal role in shaping the astrology we know today. The Greeks introduced the concept of the zodiac, a band of celestial space divided into twelve segments, each associated with specific zodiac signs and the months of the year. They also linked these signs with personality traits and characteristics. Greek philosophers like Ptolemy further refined astrological principles, emphasizing the connection between celestial movements and human destinies. This laid the foundation for modern Western astrology.

Renaissance and Modern Astrology: During the Renaissance, astrology experienced a resurgence in interest. Scholars such as Johannes Kepler and Galileo

Galilei explored the relationships between celestial bodies and their potential impact on human lives. They sought to integrate astrology with the emerging field of astronomy. In modern times, astrology has evolved and adapted to new cultural contexts, gaining widespread popularity in various societies around the world.

Throughout history, astrology has served diverse purposes, from predicting agricultural cycles in ancient civilizations to offering personal and psychological interpretations of individuals' lives in contemporary settings. Its enduring influence on human culture and belief systems reflects the enduring fascination with celestial realm and its connection to our daily lives.

Part 2: The Origins of the Zodiac Signs

Babylonian Influence: The origins of the zodiac signs can be traced back to ancient Babylonian astrology. The Babylonians were among the first to develop a systematic approach to understanding the movement of celestial bodies. Their division of the sky into twelve segments, corresponding to the twelve months of the year, laid the foundation for the zodiac as we know it. This division was primarily for agricultural and calendrical purposes, with each month associated with a specific zodiac sign. These early signs were simpler and didn't yet include symbols or attributes.

Greek Zodiac: The Greeks further refined and enhanced the Babylonian zodiac system. They introduced symbols, elements, and ruling planets for each of the zodiac signs, imbuing them with deeper meaning and personality traits.

- Symbols: The Greeks associated distinct symbols with each zodiac sign. For instance, Cancer is symbolized by the Crab, a creature with a protective shell, symbolizing the sign's nurturing and protective qualities.

- Elements: They also assigned elements to the signs, with Cancer belonging to the water element. This elemental association reflects Cancer's emotional depth and sensitivity.

- Ruling Planets: The Greeks linked each zodiac sign to specific ruling planets. Cancer is ruled by the Moon, emphasizing the sign's connection to emotions and intuition.

The Greek zodiac system added depth and symbolism to the zodiac signs, turning them into more than just markers of time but also tools for understanding human personality and destiny.

The combination of Babylonian and Greek influences has shaped the zodiac signs into the astrological system we use today, with each sign carrying its unique symbolism, elements, and ruling planets.

Part 3: The Mythological Background of Cancer

Cancer is not just a celestial sign but also a constellation with a captivating mythological background.

The Story of Cancer: In Greek mythology, Cancer is associated with the tale of the Nemean Crab. This story is intertwined with the Twelve Labors of Hercules, the renowned hero of Greek mythology.

According to the myth, Hera, the wife of Zeus and queen of the gods, sought to hinder Hercules, who was renowned for his incredible strength and heroic feats. To accomplish this, she sent a giant crab, known as the Nemean Crab or

Karkinos, to distract Hercules during his second labor.

Hercules was tasked with defeating the Nemean Lion, a powerful and invulnerable beast. While Hercules was engaged in a fierce battle with the lion, the crab approached him, attempting to pinch his foot and disrupt his efforts. However, Hercules easily dispatched the crab with a swift kick.

In recognition of the crab's bravery and dedication to the task assigned by Hera, the goddess placed the Nemean Crab in the night sky as the constellation Cancer. Thus, the crab became an enduring symbol of constancy, determination, and the protection of the home.

The mythological background of Cancer adds a layer of symbolism and depth to the astrological interpretation of this zodiac sign. The protective nature of Cancer is reflected in the story of the Nemean Crab and its loyalty to the divine will of Hera.

Cancer in Love

This chapter delves into the romantic aspects of the Cancer zodiac sign, providing insights into their approach to love, relationships, and compatibility.

Part 1: Cancer's Approach to Love

In the first section, we will explore how Cancer individuals approach love. This includes their values, priorities, and the qualities they seek in a romantic partner.

Cancer individuals are known for their deep emotional connections and their nurturing nature, which also extends to their love lives. Their approach to love is characterized by:

1. Emotional Depth: Cancer individuals value emotional intimacy and depth in their romantic relationships. They seek partners who can connect with them on an emotional level and understand their feelings.

2. Loyalty and Commitment: Cancer individuals are fiercely loyal and committed in love. They seek long-term, stable relationships and prioritize the well-being and happiness of their partners.

3. Nurturing and Care: Their nurturing qualities extend to their romantic partnerships. They often take on the role of the caregiver and are attentive to their partner's needs and emotions.

4. Sentimentality: Cancer individuals cherish romantic moments and traditions. They often create sentimental rituals and hold dear the memories they create with their partners.

5. Family Orientation: Family is of great importance to Cancer individuals. They seek partners who share their family values and are open to building a loving family unit.

6. Compatibility: Cancer individuals are often compatible with water signs like Pisces and Scorpio, as well as earth signs like Taurus and

Virgo. These signs can understand and appreciate their emotional depth.

PART 2: LOVE COMPATIBILITY for Cancer

In this section, we will explore the love compatibility of Cancer individuals with other zodiac signs. Understanding how Cancer's nurturing and emotional nature aligns with different signs is essential for a comprehensive view of their romantic dynamics.

Cancer individuals are most compatible with:

1. Pisces (February 19 - March 20): Pisces shares Cancer's emotional depth and desire for a deep emotional connection. This compatibility often results in a profound and empathetic partnership.

2. Scorpio (October 23 - November 21): Scorpio's intensity matches Cancer's emotional commitment. Both

signs value loyalty and commitment in a relationship, which can lead to a strong and passionate bond.

3. Taurus (April 20 - May 20): Taurus appreciates Cancer's nurturing qualities and provides stability in the relationship. This combination can create a harmonious and grounded partnership.

4. Virgo (August 23 - September 22): Virgo's practical and caring nature complements Cancer's emotional depth. These signs can form a supportive and nurturing bond.

5. Capricorn (December 22 - January 19): Capricorn's determination and Cancer's emotional support can create a powerful and committed partnership. Both signs value loyalty and long-term stability.

Cancer individuals may experience challenges in relationships with signs that have different approaches to emotions and commitment. However, these challenges can be overcome with open communication and understanding.

Part 3: Nurturing and Maintaining a Loving Relationship

In this section, we will explore how Cancer individuals nurture and maintain a loving relationship. Their caring and empathetic nature extends to their efforts in creating a harmonious and loving partnership.

Cancer individuals excel at:

1. Emotional Support: They provide unwavering emotional support to their partners. Cancer individuals are

attentive listeners and are quick to offer comfort and understanding in times of emotional distress.

2. Creating a Nurturing Environment: They ensure their relationship feels like a safe and nurturing space. Their homes are often warm and welcoming, providing a sense of security for their partners.

3. Traditions and Sentimentality: Cancer individuals often create romantic traditions and cherish sentimental moments in their relationships. These rituals help strengthen their emotional connection with their partners.

4. Communication: They value open and honest communication. Cancer individuals express their feelings and encourage their partners to do the same. This fosters trust and a deep emotional bond.

5. Loyalty and Commitment: Their unwavering loyalty and commitment to their partners create a stable and reliable foundation for the relationship.

6. Conflict Resolution: Cancer individuals approach conflicts with a nurturing mindset. They seek to understand and resolve issues while maintaining the emotional well-being of both partners.

7. Building a Family: Many Cancer individuals prioritize building a family with their partners. Family is a central focus for them, and they strive to create a loving and supportive family unit.

This section offers an in-depth look at how Cancer individuals contribute to the nurturing and maintenance of loving relationships. Their empathetic and caring nature creates a strong emotional connection with their partners.

Cancer in Astrology

Section 1: Explain the Role of Cancer in the Astrological Chart

Cancer is a pivotal zodiac sign in the astrological chart, and its placement holds significant influence over an individual's astrological profile. Let's break down the key aspects of Cancer's role in the astrological chart:

- Natal Chart Placement: In an astrological chart, Cancer is one of the twelve zodiac signs. The position of Cancer in an individual's natal chart reveals the position of the Sun at the time of their birth. This is commonly referred to as the Sun sign and is one of the primary components of an individual's astrological identity.

- Emotional Depth: Cancer is often associated with emotional depth. Those with Cancer prominent in their chart tend to have a strong connection to their emotions. They experience feelings on a profound level and are often in touch with their inner emotional landscape.

- Home and Family Life: Cancer is deeply connected to themes of home and family. Its placement in the astrological chart indicates an individual's approach to their home life, their family relationships, and their nurturing tendencies. Individuals with Cancer emphasized in their chart often prioritize the well-being and comfort of their family members.

• Security and Comfort: Cancer's role in the chart influences an individual's desire for emotional security and comfort. They seek environments and relationships that provide a sense of safety and emotional fulfillment.

• House Placement: In addition to its zodiac position, Cancer's role can be further defined by its placement in a specific house of the natal chart. This house placement refines the sign's influence, directing it toward specific areas of an individual's life. For example, Cancer in the 4th house would strongly influence an individual's home life, while Cancer in the 7th house might shape their approach to relationships and partnerships.

Cancer's role in the astrological chart is multi-faceted, encompassing emotional depth, nurturing tendencies, and a strong connection to home and family. Its placement provides valuable insights into an individual's personality, emotional makeup, and life preferences.

Section 2: Discuss the Influence of Cancer on Personality and Behavior

Cancer is a zodiac sign that exerts a significant influence on an individual's personality and behavior. Let's delve into the specific ways in which Cancer shapes a person's character and actions:

• Emotional Sensitivity: Cancer individuals are known for their heightened emotional sensitivity. They experience and process emotions on a deep and profound level. This emotional depth influences their behavior by making them empathetic and compassionate. They are often keenly attuned to the feelings of others and are quick to offer support and understanding.

• Nurturing Qualities: The nurturing nature of Cancer is a defining characteristic. Individuals with a strong Cancer influence tend to be natural caregivers. They take on the role of nurturers within their families and social circles, offering emotional support and protection to their loved ones. This nurturing quality extends to their behavior in relationships, where they show great care and concern for their partners.

• Family-Centric Values: Cancer's influence is particularly evident in the strong family-centered values of individuals with this sign prominent in their charts. They prioritize their families and create warm, welcoming home environments. Their behavior reflects their

commitment to family bonds and their desire to maintain a closeknit, loving family unit.

• Sentimentality: Cancer individuals are often deeply sentimental. They attach great significance to keepsakes, traditions, and cherished memories. Their behavior includes creating and cherishing sentimental rituals, celebrating important milestones, and preserving the memories that hold emotional value.

• Adaptive Behavior: Cancer individuals exhibit adaptive behavior, particularly in social situations. Their emotional intelligence enables them to navigate diverse social settings with ease. They adjust their behavior according to the emotional atmosphere, making them adept at creating a harmonious and comfortable environment for those around them.

• Home as a Sanctuary: The strong connection to home and family life also influences their behavior. They often view their homes as sanctuaries of comfort and security. Their behavior reflects their desire to create and maintain a loving, protective, and welcoming home environment.

The influence of Cancer on personality and behavior is characterized by emotional sensitivity, nurturing tendencies, family-centric values, sentimentality, adaptability, and a strong connection to home life. Understanding these traits provides valuable insights into the actions and reactions of individuals with Cancer prominent in their astrological charts.

Section 3: Explore Compatibility and Relationships with Other Signs

In this section, we will delve into how individuals with the Cancer zodiac sign interact with individuals of other zodiac signs in terms of compatibility and relationships. This exploration provides valuable insights into the dynamics of their relationships with various signs.

• Compatible Signs: Cancer individuals are often most compatible with specific zodiac signs due to shared qualities and complementary traits. These signs appreciate and understand Cancer's emotional depth and nurturing tendencies. The compatible signs include:

• Pisces: Pisces shares Cancer's emotional depth and desire for a deep emotional connection. Both signs are intuitive and empathetic, making for a profound and supportive partnership.

• Scorpio: Scorpio's intensity matches Cancer's emotional commitment. Both signs value loyalty and commitment in a relationship, leading to a passionate and enduring bond.

- Taurus: Taurus appreciates Cancer's nurturing qualities and provides stability in the relationship. This combination can create a harmonious and grounded partnership.

- Virgo: Virgo's practical and caring nature complements Cancer's emotional depth. Together, they can form a supportive and nurturing bond.

- Capricorn: Capricorn's determination and Cancer's emotional support can create a powerful and committed partnership. Both signs value loyalty and long-term stability.

- Challenges with Some Signs: While Cancer individuals can form strong bonds with compatible signs, they may face challenges in relationships with signs that have different approaches to emotions and commitment. These challenges can be overcome with open communication and understanding. For example, signs that emphasize independence and logic, such as Aries or Aquarius, may require more patience and effort in finding common ground with Cancer.

Exploring compatibility and relationships with other signs helps individuals with Cancer prominent in their charts navigate their social and romantic in-

Reactions more effectively. It provides insights into the strengths and potential challenges they may encounter in their relationships.

Personality Traits and Characteristics

SECTION 1: DETAIL THE Positive Traits of Cancer Individuals

Cancer individuals possess a rich tapestry of positive personality traits that make them remarkable and endearing. Here's an in-depth exploration of these traits:

• Emotional Depth: Cancer individuals are known for their profound emotional depth. They experience and process emotions on a deeper level than many other signs. This emotional intelligence allows them to connect with others in a way that is empathetic, understanding, and supportive. They have the capacity to feel not only their emotions but also the emotions of those around them, making them compassionate and caring friends and partners.

• Nurturing Nature: One of Cancer's standout positive traits is their innate nurturing nature. They have a natural instinct to care for and protect their loved ones. Whether it's in their role as parents, friends, or partners, Cancer individuals create a warm and loving atmosphere. They excel at providing emotional support and ensuring the well-being of those in their lives. Their nurturing qualities foster a sense of security and comfort in their relationships and homes.

• Loyalty and Commitment: Loyalty is a cornerstone of Cancer's personality. They place tremendous value on loyalty and commitment in their relationships. Once they form deep emotional bonds, Cancer individuals are unwavering in their dedication and support. They stand by their loved ones through good times and bad, making them dependable and trustworthy companions.

• Intuitive: Cancer individuals possess a strong sense of intuition. They have a remarkable ability to read the emotions and needs of others, even when unspoken. Their intuition guides them in making considerate and empathetic decisions in their interactions with people. This sensitivity to the emotional subtleties of others makes them attentive and responsive partners and friends.

• Creativity: Many Cancer individuals have a creative spirit that they express in various forms, whether it's through art, music, writing, or other imaginative endeavors. Their creativity adds a unique dimension to their personalities. They often excel in fields that require a deep connection to emotions and the ability to convey those feelings through creative expression.

• Adaptability: Cancer individuals are adaptable. They possess the capacity to navigate various social settings and adjust their behavior according to the emotional atmosphere. This adaptability contributes to their ability to create harmonious and comfortable environments for themselves and those around them. They are adept at connecting with a diverse range of people due to their ability to respond to varying emotional dynamics.

These positive traits collectively make Cancer individuals compassionate, nurturing, and dependable.

Their emotional depth, loyalty, and intuitive understanding of others create strong, loving relationships and supportive home environments. Their creativity and adaptability add a layer of richness to their personalities, making them engaging and empathetic individuals to be around.

Section 2: Discuss the Challenges and Negative Traits

While Cancer individuals possess numerous positive traits, it's essential to understand the challenges and negative traits associated with this zodiac sign:

- Moodiness: One of the key challenges for Cancer individuals is their susceptibility to mood swings and emotional fluctuations. Their deep emotional nature can lead to periods of moodiness and

heightened sensitivity to their surroundings. They may experience emotional highs and lows more intensely than other signs.

- Overprotectiveness: Cancer's nurturing qualities can sometimes translate into overprotectiveness, especially in their relationships with loved ones. While they genuinely care and want to safeguard the well-being of others, this trait can become stifling if not balanced effectively. Overprotectiveness can unintentionally limit the freedom and independence of those they care about.

- Difficulty in Letting Go: Cancer individuals may struggle with letting go of past hurts or grievances. Their emotional depth can lead to long-lasting emotional attachments to negative experiences. They may hold onto grudges or dwell on past issues, making it challenging to move forward and find resolution.

• Introversion: Some Cancer individuals lean towards introversion and may find comfort in the close-knit circle of their homes and families. While this trait allows them to create secure and nurturing environments, it can also limit their exposure to new experiences, people, and opportunities. Their introverted tendencies may hinder personal growth and exploration beyond their comfort zone.

• Avoidance of Conflict: Cancer individuals often avoid conflict to maintain peace and harmony. While this may seem like a positive trait, it can sometimes lead to suppressing their own needs or feelings. Avoiding necessary conflicts can prevent the resolution of issues and may result in unresolved tensions in their relationships.

Understanding these challenges and negative traits is vital for both Cancer individuals and those who interact with them. By recognizing and addressing these aspects, individuals with Cancer prominent in their charts can navigate their emotional landscape more effectively and foster healthier, more balanced relationships.

Real-Life Examples of Famous Cancer Personalities

Princess Diana (July 1): Princess Diana, one of the most beloved figures in modern history, was born on July 1. She exemplified the positive traits of Cancer individuals, such as emotional depth and nurturing qualities. Diana was renowned for her genuine compassion and empathy towards those in need. Her commitment to humanitarian causes and her ability to connect with people emotionally made her a beloved and respected figure worldwide. Her nurturing and caring nature was evident in her role as a mother and her dedication to charitable work.

● Tom Hanks (July 9): As an actor, Tom Hanks, born on July 9, embodies the nurturing and relatable qualities often associated with Cancer individuals. He is known for his ability to convey deep emotions and create empathetic characters in his roles. His performances are a testament to his emotional range and his capacity to connect with audiences on an emotional level. Tom Hanks has a warm and relatable on-screen presence that mirrors Cancer's nurturing nature.

● Meryl Streep (June 22): Meryl Streep, born on June 22, is often regarded as one of the most celebrated actors of our time. She showcases the adaptability and emotional depth that are common traits of Cancer individuals. Her versatility as an actor allows her to convincingly portray a wide range of characters, each with their unique emotional landscapes. Meryl Streep's ability to convey complex emotions and create empathetic, multi-dimensional characters has earned her numerous accolades.

These real-life examples of famous Cancer personalities demonstrate the diversity and impact of this zodiac sign. They have left a lasting legacy through their contributions in various fields and have showcased the positive traits of Cancer, such as emotional depth, nurturing qualities, and adaptability.

Career and Life Path of Cancer

Section 1: Discuss the Career Preferences and Strengths of Cancer Individuals

Cancer individuals exhibit specific career preferences and strengths that align with their unique personality traits and make them valuable contributors in various professions. Let's explore these traits in greater detail:

• Career Preferences: Cancer individuals often gravitate towards careers that allow them to express their nurturing nature and emotional depth. Their strong desire to care for and support others makes them excel in professions where they can make a positive impact on people's lives. Here are some career preferences commonly associated with Cancer individuals:

• Healthcare: Cancer individuals are drawn to healthcare professions, such as nursing, counseling, or psychology, where they can offer emotional support and care to patients and clients. Their empathetic nature and deep emotional understanding make them ideal healthcare providers.

• Teaching and Education: Education is another field where Cancer individuals thrive. Their nurturing qualities make them exceptional teachers, mentors, and educators.

They excel at creating a safe and supportive learning environment for students.

- Counseling and Social Work: The field of counseling and social work is a natural fit for Cancer individuals due to their strong emotional intelligence and empathy. They can help individuals navigate through their emotional challenges and provide the support needed to overcome obstacles.

- Parenting and Childcare: Many Cancer individuals are excellent parents and caregivers. Their natural instinct to nurture and protect their loved ones extends to their role as parents, making them loving and caring guardians.

- Creative and Artistic Fields: Cancer's emotional depth often drives them toward creative and artistic pursuits. They may find fulfillment in careers related to art, music, writing, or other imaginative endeavors that allow them to express their deep emotions and connect with audiences on an emotional level.

- Home-Related Professions: Given their strong connection to home life, some Cancer individuals may excel in careers related to real estate, interior design, or home-based businesses. Their nurturing qualities can contribute to creating welcoming and comfortable home environments.

- Strengths in the Workplace: Cancer individuals bring a unique set of strengths to the workplace, which are shaped by their personality traits:

- Emotional Intelligence: Their emotional depth and empathy are valuable assets in the workplace. They excel in roles that require understanding and managing emotions, making them excellent team members and leaders.

- Loyalty and Commitment: Cancer individuals are known for their unwavering loyalty and commitment. This dedication translates into a strong work ethic and reliability. They are dependable and are often trusted to complete tasks and projects with diligence.

- Adaptability: Their adaptability allows them to navigate diverse work environments effectively. They can adjust to changing circumstances and provide support in various roles, making them versatile team members.

Empathetic Leadership: In leadership roles, Cancer individuals often lead with empathy and a focus on the well-being of their team members. They create supportive and nurturing work environments that foster collaboration and productivity.

Understanding the career preferences and strengths of Cancer individuals provides valuable insights for both their personal career choices and their potential contributions to the workplace. These traits, such as empathy, commitment, and adaptability, make them valuable assets in a wide range of professions.

Section 2: Explain How Their Personality Traits Influence Their Life Path

The personality traits of Cancer individuals play a profound role in shaping their life path. These traits influence their choices, relationships, and overall life journey. Let's explore how these traits guide their life path:

• Emotional Depth: Cancer individuals are known for their profound emotional depth. This emotional richness influences their life path by guiding them towards experiences and careers that allow them to connect with others on a deep emotional level. They prioritize relationships, family, and emotional well-being in their lives. Their innate capacity to feel emotions intensely can lead them towards paths that involve understanding and addressing emotional needs, both their own and those of others. This often results in choices that prioritize emotional well-being, empathy, and emotional connection.

• Nurturing Nature: The nurturing nature of Cancer individuals is a driving force in their life path. They are drawn towards roles and experiences that involve taking care of others. This extends to their role as parents, caregivers, and providers of emotional support within their families and social circles. Their life path often leads them to embrace opportunities to care for and protect their loved ones. Their journey may be deeply intertwined with creating and maintaining a loving, nurturing environment for those they hold dear.

• Loyalty and Commitment: Loyalty and commitment are foundational traits for Cancer individuals. These traits guide their life path by leading them towards long-term relationships, both in their personal and professional lives. Whether it's a romantic partnership, a career choice, or a commitment to a cause, Cancer individuals invest deeply and persistently. Their dedication to their chosen path and their enduring commitment to their goals contribute to their achievements and the stability of their life journey.

• Creativity: Many Cancer individuals have a creative spirit, and this creativity often plays a significant role in shaping their life path. They may be drawn to artistic, imaginative, or emotionally expressive fields where they can express their deep emotions and connect with audiences on an emotional level. Their creativity adds a unique dimension to their life journey, allowing them to pursue careers and experiences that involve self-expression and emotional depth.

• Adaptability: The adaptability of Cancer individuals ensures that they can navigate life's challenges and changes effectively. This trait guides their life path by allowing them to adjust to new circumstances and seize opportunities. Whether facing personal changes, career shifts, or unexpected challenges, their adaptability ensures that they can navigate the complexities of life with resilience. Their journey may involve embracing diverse experiences, personal growth, and an openness to new opportunities.

The combination of these personality traits—emotional depth, nurturing nature, loyalty, creativity, and adaptability—results in a unique life path for Cancer individuals. Their choices, relationships, and experiences are often marked by a strong focus on emotional well-being, deep connections, and a commitment to nurturing those around them. These traits influence both their personal and professional journeys and guide them towards careers and experiences that align with their innate qualities.

Section 3: Provide Examples of Successful Cancer Individuals in Various Fields

1. Nelson Mandela (July 18): Nelson Mandela, born under the Cancer sign, was a remarkable figure in the political world. He achieved significant success as a global statesman and anti-apartheid revolutionary. His nurturing nature and dedication to the cause of equality made him a symbol of resilience and reconciliation. He played a pivotal role in the struggle for justice and human rights, ultimately becoming the President of South Africa and working to end apartheid.

2. Selena Gomez (July 22): Selena Gomez, a Cancer, is a well-known figure in the entertainment industry. She is a successful actress, singer, and producer. Her emotional depth and creativity have contributed to her success in both music and acting. Selena Gomez has a strong presence in the world of entertainment, and her work showcases the emotional depth and expressive qualities often associated with Cancer individuals.

3. Malala Yousafzai (July 12): Malala Yousafzai, also a Cancer, is renowned for her advocacy for girls' education. Her commitment to social justice and her empathetic nature have been driving forces in her successful life path as an education activist. She became the youngest-ever Nobel Prize laureate for her efforts to promote education for girls and her work in advocating for gender equality.

These examples illustrate how Cancer individuals can find success in a wide range of fields, from politics and entertainment to social activism. Their emotional depth, nurturing qualities, and dedication guide them towards paths that allow them to make a positive impact on society and connect with others on a deep emotional level.

The Challenges and Growth of

Cancer

SECTION 1: ADDRESS Common Challenges Faced by Cancer Individuals

Cancer individuals, like individuals of any zodiac sign, may encounter specific challenges in their lives. Here, we'll address common challenges that Cancer individuals often face:

1. Mood Swings and Emotional Fluctuations: Cancer individuals are known for their deep emotional nature. However, this emotional depth can lead to mood swings and emotional fluctuations. These mood swings may affect their daily lives and relationships, causing moments of heightened sensitivity or emotional turbulence. Learning to manage and balance these emotions is essential for their emotional well-being and the harmony of their relationships.

2. Overprotectiveness: Cancer individuals have a strong nurturing nature and a desire to care for their loved ones. While this is a positive trait, it can sometimes lead to overprotectiveness. They may become overly concerned about the well-being of their family and friends to the extent that it restricts the independence of those they care

about. Striking a balance between care and allowing others the freedom to make their own choices can be a challenge.

3. Difficulty in Letting Go: Cancer individuals may struggle with letting go of past hurts or grievances. Their emotional depth makes it challenging for them to move on from negative experiences. This difficulty in letting go can lead to holding onto grudges, which can be detrimental to personal well-being and relationships. Learning to forgive, release past grievances, and focus on the present is a growth opportunity.

89

4. Introversion: Some Cancer individuals lean towards introversion, finding comfort in the familiarity of their homes and close-knit social circles. While this introverted nature offers a sense of security, it can also limit their exposure to new experiences, people, and opportunities. Overcoming this introverted tendency to explore new horizons and engage with the world beyond their comfort zone can be a challenge.

5. Avoidance of Conflict: Cancer individuals often avoid conflict to maintain peace and harmony. While this may seem like a positive trait, it can sometimes lead to suppressing their own needs or feelings. Avoiding necessary conflicts can prevent the resolution of issues and may result in unresolved tensions in their relationships.

Addressing these common challenges is essential for personal growth and emotional well-being. Learning to manage emotions, strike a balance between nurturing and independence, practice forgiveness, embrace new experiences, and engage in constructive conflict resolution are steps that can help Cancer individuals overcome these challenges and lead fulfilling lives.

Section 2: Offer Guidance on Personal Growth and Self-Improvement

Cancer individuals can embark on a journey of personal growth and self-improvement by addressing specific areas of focus. Here's guidance tailored to their zodiac sign:

• Emotional Management: To enhance personal growth, it's essential for Cancer individuals to focus on emotional management. This involves gaining better control over mood swings and emotional fluctuations. Here are steps for emotional management:

- Self-Awareness: Start by becoming more self-aware of your emotions. Practice mindfulness, meditation, or journaling to understand your emotional patterns and triggers. This self-awareness is the first step in managing your emotions effectively.

- Expression, Not Suppression: Instead of suppressing your emotions, learn healthy ways to express them. Talk to a trusted friend, family member, or therapist when you're experiencing intense emotions. Artistic expression, like painting or writing, can also provide an outlet for your feelings.

- Seeking Support: Don't hesitate to seek support when needed. If mood swings or emotional fluctuations are affecting your daily life, consulting with a mental health professional can provide valuable guidance and strategies for emotional management.

- Balancing Nurturing Instincts: Cancer individuals often have strong nurturing instincts, which can be both a strength and a challenge. To achieve self-improvement in this area, consider the following:

- Establish Boundaries: Recognize when your nurturing instincts may lead to overprotectiveness. Establish healthy boundaries in your relationships to allow loved ones their independence while still providing support.

- Encourage Independence: Encourage the independence and selfsufficiency of those you care for.

This can involve offering guidance rather than taking control and allowing them to make their own decisions.

• Letting Go and Forgiveness: To foster personal growth, work on letting go of past hurts and grievances. Forgiveness is a powerful tool for emotional well-being. Here's how to practice forgiveness:

• Acceptance: Accept that holding onto grudges only harms your own well-being. Realize that forgiveness is not about condoning the actions of others but freeing yourself from the burden of negative emotions.

• Release and Heal: Release the emotional attachments to past grievances. Engage in healing activities, such as meditation or therapy, to work through any lingering emotional pain. Focus on the present and future rather than dwelling on the past.

•Extroverted Engagement: If you have introverted tendencies, personal growth can involve challenging yourself to engage more with the external world. Here are steps to achieve self-improvement in this area:

• Step Out of Your Comfort Zone: Seek new experiences and engage in social activities that may push you beyond your comfort zone. This can include attending events, joining clubs, or trying new hobbies.

• Expand Social Circles: Make an effort to expand your social and professional circles. Networking and building connections with a diverse range of people can offer new perspectives and opportunities for growth.

• Effective Conflict Resolution: To achieve self-improvement in the area of conflict resolution, focus on these steps:

• Open Communication: Develop effective communication skills for addressing conflicts. Speak openly and honestly with others about your needs and concerns.

• Active Listening: Practice active listening by truly understanding the perspectives of others. This can facilitate the resolution of conflicts and strengthen relationships.

• Conflict Resolution Strategies: Learn and implement constructive conflict resolution strategies. This may involve compromise, negotiation, and finding win-win solutions to issues.

Engaging in personal growth and self-improvement is a continuous journey, and these guidance points are tailored to help Cancer individuals navigate their unique challenges and strengths. It's important to remember that personal growth is a process that requires patience and self-compassion.

Section 3: Discuss How to Harness Their Strengths and Overcome Weaknesses

Cancer individuals can harness their strengths and work on overcoming their weaknesses to lead fulfilling lives. Here's guidance on how to do this:

Strength: Emotional Depth

- Harness: Utilize your emotional depth as a strength. Your capacity to connect with others on a deep emotional level can be a valuable asset in your personal and professional life. Empathy and understanding can create profound relationships and connections with others.

Weakness: Mood Swings and Emotional Fluctuations

- Overcome: To address mood swings and emotional fluctuations, focus on emotional management. Develop self-awareness of your emotional patterns and triggers. Seek healthy ways to express your emotions, whether through creative outlets, talking to trusted individuals, or seeking professional help when needed.

Strength: Nurturing Qualities

- Harness: Balance your nurturing instincts by providing support to your loved ones while allowing them the freedom to make their own choices. This balance enhances your relationships and fosters personal growth. Recognize that your care and support can be a tremendous strength.

Weakness: Overprotectiveness

- Overcome: Avoid overprotectiveness by setting healthy boundaries in your relationships. Encourage the independence and self-sufficiency of those you care for. Offer guidance and support without stifling their choices.

Strength: Loyalty and Commitment

- Harness: Your unwavering loyalty and commitment are strengths that can lead to long-lasting and meaningful relationships. Use your dedication to achieve personal and professional goals.

Weakness: Difficulty in Letting Go

- Overcome: To overcome difficulty in letting go, focus on forgiveness and release. Understand that holding onto past hurts or grievances can hinder your personal well-being. Forgiveness is a powerful tool for your emotional growth and peace of mind.

Strength: Creativity

- Harness: Many Cancer individuals have a creative spirit. Embrace this creativity as a strength that allows you to express your deep emotions and connect with audiences on an emotional level. Engage in creative pursuits and endeavors that showcase your imaginative abilities.

Weakness: Introversion

- Overcome: To address introversion, challenge yourself to step out of your comfort zone. Engage in new experiences, expand your social and professional circles, and seek opportunities that allow you to grow and connect with a diverse range of people.

Strength: Adaptability

- Harness: Your adaptability is a valuable asset that enables you to navigate life's challenges and changes effectively. Embrace change, open yourself to new opportunities, and adjust to evolving circumstances with resilience.

Weakness: Avoidance of Conflict

• Overcome: Effective conflict resolution involves open and honest communication. Develop skills for addressing conflicts constructively. Focus on understanding the perspectives of others, and practice active listening. Implement conflict resolution strategies that can lead to positive outcomes.

Harnessing strengths and working on overcoming weaknesses is a continual journey of personal growth and self-improvement. By recognizing your unique qualities and addressing the areas that present challenges, you can lead a more fulfilling and balanced life.

Section 1: Explain the Connection Between Cancer and the Moon

The connection between the Cancer zodiac sign and the Moon is deeply ingrained in the astrological and mystical world. Cancer is often referred to as the "Moon Child," and this connection is characterized by several significant aspects:

1. Emotional Sensitivity: Cancer individuals are known for their heightened emotional sensitivity. This trait is closely tied to the influence of the Moon, which represents emotions, intuition, and the subconscious mind. The Moon governs the tides, and in a similar fashion, Cancer individuals experience emotional tides. They possess a remarkable ability to understand, feel, and express their emotions with great depth.

2. Nurturing and Protectiveness: The Moon is often associated with nurturing, caregiving, and protection. Cancer individuals exhibit these qualities in abundance. They have a natural inclination to care for and protect their loved ones, mirroring the Moon's role as a gentle, guiding force in the night sky. This nurturing instinct is one of the hallmarks of their personality.

3. Cycles and Timing: The Moon's phases and cycles have a significant impact on Cancer individuals. Lunar phases, such as the New Moon and Full Moon, are moments of heightened importance for them. They often recognize the importance of timing and cycles in various aspects of their lives, including relationships, career, and personal growth. The lunar phases serve as guides for their decision-making and actions.

4. Intuitive Wisdom: The Moon is associated with intuitive wisdom, and Cancer individuals possess an innate sense of intuition. They often rely on their gut feelings and inner guidance to make decisions. This intuitive wisdom, deeply rooted in their lunar connection, allows them to navigate life with an uncanny sense of what is right and true.

96

In summary, the connection between Cancer and the Moon is profound and multifaceted. It shapes their emotional depth, nurturing qualities, sense of timing, and intuitive wisdom. This lunar connection is a fundamental aspect of their personality and plays a significant role in influencing their thoughts, emotions, and actions.

Section 2: Discuss How Lunar Phases Impact Cancer Individuals

Lunar phases hold special significance for Cancer individuals due to their strong connection to the Moon. Here's a breakdown of how different lunar phases may influence them:

1. New Moon: The New Moon is a time of fresh beginnings and setting intentions. For Cancer individuals, this phase often marks a period of renewed motivation and a desire to initiate positive changes in their lives. They may be particularly attuned to setting emotional goals and nurturing their connections with loved ones during this time.

2. Full Moon: The Full Moon can have an intense impact on Cancer individuals. They may experience heightened emotional sensitivity during this phase. This

can manifest as deeper feelings and a heightened awareness of their emotions. It's essential for Cancer individuals to manage emotional fluctuations during this time and to use the Full Moon's energy for increased creativity and self-expression.

3. Waxing Moon: The Waxing Moon phase is a time of growth and progress. Cancer individuals may find themselves motivated to work toward their goals and make significant strides in their personal and professional lives. It's an ideal time for them to nurture their relationships and explore new opportunities.

4. Waning Moon: The Waning Moon phase encourages reflection and letting go. Cancer individuals may feel a pull to release what no longer serves them, whether that's old emotional baggage, unproductive patterns, or negative experiences. It's a time for decluttering their emotional world and preparing for a new cycle.

5. Eclipses: Eclipses, which occur during specific lunar phases, can have a profound impact on Cancer individuals. These events may bring transformative experiences, significant changes in their life path, and a deeper understanding of their emotions and purpose. Cancer individuals should pay close attention to eclipses, as they often mark pivotal moments in their lives.

Lunar phases serve as guides for Cancer individuals, helping them align their actions and intentions with the cosmic rhythm. The Moon's influence is deeply intertwined with their emotional depth and nurturing qualities, making these phases especially meaningful for their personal and spiritual growth.

Section 3: Explore the Emotional Depth Associated with This Sign

Cancer individuals are renowned for their exceptional emotional depth, and this quality is a defining aspect of their personality. Here, we'll explore the facets of this emotional depth:

1. Empathy: Cancer individuals possess a remarkable sense of empathy. They can easily connect with the emotions of others, and their ability to understand and share the feelings of those around them is one of their greatest strengths. This empathy allows them to provide comfort and support to friends, family, and even strangers in times of need.

2. Intuitive Emotional Understanding: Their emotional depth is further enhanced by their intuitive emotional understanding. They have a unique knack for sensing and interpreting the unspoken feelings of those they interact with. This intuitive quality enables them to offer guidance, solace, and compassion when it's needed the most.

3. Connection to Home and Family: Cancer individuals often exhibit a deep emotional connection to their home and family. They prioritize the bonds they share with loved ones and work tirelessly to create warm, nurturing environments for those they care about. Their home is a sanctuary where emotions are valued and cherished.

4. Emotional Resilience: Despite their emotional sensitivity, Cancer individuals display emotional resilience. They can weather life's challenges with grace and determination, using their emotional depth

as a source of strength. Their capacity to bounce back from adversity is a testament to their inner fortitude.

5. Emotional Expression: Cancer individuals are skilled at expressing their emotions. They use various means, such as art, writing, or heartfelt conversations, to articulate their feelings. Their emotional expression is a window into their souls, allowing others to connect with the profound emotions that reside within them.

6. Vulnerability and Authenticity: They are unafraid to be vulnerable and authentic in their interactions. This honesty about their feelings fosters genuine connections with others and allows them to build relationships based on trust and understanding.

7. Emotional Bonding: Cancer individuals tend to form deep emotional bonds with the people in their lives. These connections are enduring and significant. They often carry a strong sense of responsibility towards those they love and prioritize their emotional well-being.

The emotional depth associated with Cancer individuals is a gift that enriches their lives and the lives of those they touch. It allows them to create profound relationships, offer support and comfort, and navigate the complex landscape of human emotions with sensitivity and grace.

Astrology and Modern Life

───

Section 1: Discuss the Relevance of Astrology in the Modern World

Astrology remains relevant in the modern world for several compelling reasons:

1. Self-Discovery: In an era where self-awareness and personal growth are highly valued, astrology serves as a powerful tool for selfdiscovery. Individuals turn to their birth charts to gain insights into their personality, strengths, and potential challenges. The astrological framework offers a unique and holistic perspective on one's identity, helping individuals better understand themselves.

2. Guidance: The complexity of modern life often leaves individuals seeking guidance in various aspects of their lives. Astrology provides a source of guidance based on cosmic principles. Whether individuals are making career decisions, navigating relationships, or pursuing personal development, astrology offers recommendations and insights tailored to their unique birth charts. It helps individuals align their choices with the cosmic rhythms.

3. Spirituality: In a world where spirituality takes diverse forms, astrology offers a spiritual outlet for many. It allows individuals to connect with the cosmos and explore the mysteries of the universe through the lens of their astrological signs and birth charts. Astrology can be a

deeply spiritual and reflective practice that encourages a connection with the divine, even for those who may not adhere to traditional religious beliefs.

4. Relationships: The dynamics of relationships have evolved in the digital age. Astrology plays a significant role in how people approach relationships. Compatibility analyses based on zodiac signs help individuals make informed choices about romantic partners, friends, and even business associates. Astrology provides a framework for understanding the dynamics of various relationships and can be a valuable tool for personal and professional connections.

5. Timing and Cycles: Understanding the timing of events and recognizing natural cycles are crucial in modern life. Astrology, with its emphasis on planetary movements, lunar phases, and the zodiac,

offers insights into the timing of significant life events and opportunities. It helps individuals make well-timed decisions, plan strategically, and adapt to the ebb and flow of life's challenges and blessings.

The relevance of astrology in the modern world is multifaceted. It offers individuals a path to self-awareness, a source of guidance, a connection to spirituality, a lens for understanding relationships, and a tool for recognizing the importance of timing and cycles. As the world continues to change and evolve, astrology adapts and remains a valuable resource for those seeking insight, meaning, and direction.

Section 2: Explore Horoscopes, Astrology Apps, and Popular Culture References

In the modern world, astrology has expanded its reach through various platforms, including horoscopes, astrology apps, and integration into popular culture. Here's a closer look at these aspects:

1. Horoscopes: Horoscopes have long been a popular way for individuals to access astrological insights. They are regularly featured in newspapers, magazines, and online publications. Horoscopes offer daily, weekly, or monthly astrological predictions and guidance for each zodiac sign. Many individuals turn to horoscopes for a quick glimpse into what the future may hold and for guidance in their daily lives.

2. Astrology Apps: The digital age has ushered in a new era for astrology with the rise of astrology apps. These apps provide individuals with personalized horoscopes, birth chart interpretations, and astrological insights at their fingertips. Users can access their astrological information with ease, making astrology more accessible and interactive. These apps often provide tailored recommendations based on the user's unique birth chart, offering guidance in areas like

love, career, and personal development.

3. Popular Culture References: Astrology has become deeply intertwined with popular culture. It frequently appears in movies, TV shows, music, literature, and social media. Celebrities often openly discuss their zodiac signs and birth charts, contributing to the normalization of astrology in mainstream culture. Astrological references are woven into the fabric of entertainment and art, adding layers of meaning and depth to creative works.

4. Astrology in Social Media: Social media platforms, such as Twitter, Instagram, and TikTok, have become hubs for astrology enthusiasts. Astrologers and enthusiasts share daily horoscopes, birth chart insights, and astrological advice to large followings. Astrology on social media has created a vibrant and accessible community where individuals can engage with their astrological signs and connect with like-minded people.

5. Astrological Memes and Humor: Astrology has also found a place in humor and memes on the internet. Light-hearted astrological memes playfully poke fun at the traits and quirks associated with each zodiac sign. These memes offer a relatable and entertaining take on the zodiac, making astrology accessible and enjoyable for a wide audience.

The expansion of astrology into horoscopes, astrology apps, and popular culture has made it more accessible and relatable to people from all walks of life. It serves as a bridge between the mystical and the everyday, offering insights, entertainment, and a sense of belonging within a broader community of astrology enthusiasts.

Section 3: Address the Skepticism and Belief in Astrology Today

In the contemporary world, astrology is met with a spectrum of attitudes and beliefs. Here's a closer look at the range of perspectives regarding astrology:

Skepticism:

Skepticism regarding astrology is marked by doubt and questioning of its validity as a science. Skeptics often raise the following points:

● Lack of Scientific Basis: Skeptics argue that astrology lacks a scientific basis. They emphasize that the celestial positions of stars and planets do not exert direct influence on human behavior or events on Earth.

● Confirmation Bias: Skeptics attribute the perceived accuracy of astrological readings to confirmation bias. They argue that people tend to remember the hits and forget the misses, leading to a skewed perception of astrology's accuracy.

● Forer Effect: The Forer effect, also known as the Barnum effect, is often cited by skeptics. It refers to the tendency of individuals to interpret vague and general statements as highly personalized and accurate. Skeptics argue that astrology relies on such statements to make broad claims.

Belief and Practice:

On the other end of the spectrum are individuals who genuinely believe in and practice astrology. Their beliefs are characterized by the following aspects:

●Personal Significance: Believers find personal significance in their astrological signs and birth charts. They view these as valuable tools for self-awareness and personal growth. Astrology serves as a source of guidance and understanding in their lives.

● Relationships: Many individuals use astrology as a means to explore compatibility in relationships. They believe that astrological insights can provide guidance in choosing romantic partners and nurturing existing relationships.

● Spirituality: For some, astrology is a deeply spiritual practice. It connects them with the cosmos and offers a sense of belonging in the

universe. They view their astrological signs as a window to a higher cosmic order.

● Timing and Cycles: Believers in astrology often appreciate the insights it provides into timing and life cycles. They see astrology as a valuable tool for planning and decision-making based on cosmic rhythms.

Middle Ground:

Some individuals occupy a middle ground, acknowledging both the skepticism and belief in astrology. They may not adhere to astrology as an absolute predictor of events but find value in it as a tool for self-reflection and personal growth.

The coexistence of skepticism and belief in astrology in the modern world is reflective of the complex and evolving nature of this practice. It demonstrates that astrology continues to be a topic of interest, debate, and exploration, adapting to the diverse needs and perspectives of individuals in today's society.

Turn-Ons"

———

Emotional Connection:

- Cancer individuals are known for their deep emotional nature. They value partners who can understand and connect with their feelings on a profound level.

- They appreciate conversations that delve into their emotions and create a strong emotional bond in the relationship.

- A partner who can empathize with their moods and emotional ups and downs is highly attractive to Cancerians.

Home and Family:

- Family and home life are of paramount importance to Cancer individuals. They are naturally drawn to those who share their love for creating a warm and nurturing home environment.

- Dates that involve spending quality time at home, participating in family traditions, or bonding over shared domestic activities are highly appealing to Cancer individuals.

- Their ideal partner understands and appreciates the significance of home and family in their life.

Thoughtfulness:

- Cancerians are deeply touched by thoughtful gestures and acts of kindness. They find it attractive when a partner goes out of their way to consider their well-being and happiness.

- Surprises, whether big or small, that show a genuine consideration for their feelings and needs can be a significant turn-on for Cancer individuals.

- Thoughtful gestures make them feel loved and valued, creating a strong emotional connection in the relationship.

Turn-Offs

●Cancer individuals value emotional connections and can be turned off by partners who are dismissive of their feelings or show a lack of empathy.

● Insensitivity, emotional distance, or failing to acknowledge their emotional needs can be major turn-offs for Cancerians.

Impersonal Approach:

● Cancerians are highly attuned to personal connections and may be put off by partners who keep things strictly business or fail to express warmth and affection.

●Superficial interactions, lack of emotional depth, or treating the relationship as a mere transaction can be a turn-off for Cancer individuals.

Unpredictable Behavior:

● Cancer individuals prefer stability and security in their relationships. They may be turned off by partners who exhibit unpredictable behavior or frequent mood swings.

● Inconsistency and unreliability can lead to feelings of discomfort and insecurity in a relationship with a Cancer individual.

Lack of Appreciation for Family:

● Family holds great importance for Cancerians, and they may be turned off by partners who do not prioritize family or fail to understand their strong family ties.

●Disinterest in family gatherings or a lack of support for their family values can be a turn-off for Cancer individuals.

Neglect of Home Life:

● Cancer individuals thrive in a nurturing home environment. They may be turned off by partners who neglect their domestic responsibilities or show disinterest in home life.

● Lack of enthusiasm for creating a cozy home or shared domestic activities can be a source of frustration for Cancerians.

Gifts for Cancer individuals:

1. Personalized Keepsakes: Cancerians cherish sentimental gifts, so personalized keepsakes like custom jewelry, engraved photo frames, or monogrammed items are meaningful choices.

2. Home Decor: Gifts that enhance their home, such as scented candles, cozy throw blankets, or decorative items, appeal to their love for creating a comfortable living space.

3. Cookware and Kitchen Gadgets: Cancerians often enjoy cooking and nurturing their loved ones. Quality cookware, unique kitchen gadgets, or a cookbook from their favorite chef can be appreciated.

4. Handwritten Letters: Cancer individuals value heartfelt expressions of love and emotion. A handwritten letter or a journal where they can jot down their thoughts is a thoughtful and personal gift.

5. Family Portraits: A professionally taken family portrait or a photo album filled with cherished memories can touch their hearts and celebrate their love for family.

6. Gemstones: Moonstone and pearls are associated with the Cancer zodiac sign. Jewelry featuring these gemstones, like moonstone pendants or pearl earrings, can be treasured gifts.

7. Spa or Wellness Gifts: Cancerians appreciate self-care, so spa vouchers, relaxation-themed gifts, or wellness subscriptions can help them unwind and de-stress.

8. Homemade Treats: Baking or cooking homemade treats, especially their favorite comfort foods, shows your love and thoughtfulness.

9. Family Gatherings: Plan a family get-together or a special dinner to celebrate their birthday or a significant occasion. Cancer individuals love spending quality time with loved ones.

10. A Memory Book: Create a scrapbook or a memory book filled with photos and mementos of your shared experiences and moments together.

11. Plants and Flowers: Houseplants or a bouquet of their favorite

flowers can brighten up their living space and add a touch of nature to their home.

12. Music and Playlist: A playlist of their favorite songs or concert tickets to see a beloved artist can be a delightful gift, as Cancerians often have a strong connection to music.

W

hen choosing gifts for Cancer individuals, consider their sentimental and nurturing nature, as well as their love for home and family. Personal and meaningful gifts that show you understand their emotional depth are likely to be greatly appreciated.

Adversaries to Cancer:

―――

Cancer individuals, like any other zodiac sign, may find it challenging to get along with certain signs due to differences in personality and preferences. Here are some zodiac signs that can be considered adversaries or less compatible with Cancer:

1. Aries (March 21 - April 19): Aries is known for their independent and adventurous nature, which can clash with Cancer's desire for emotional security and stability. Cancer may find Aries too impulsive and impatient at times.

2. Libra (September 23 - October 22): Libra's need for balance and harmony can sometimes conflict with Cancer's emotional intensity. Cancer may perceive Libra as indecisive or detached when it comes to addressing deeper emotional issues.

3. Capricorn (December 22 - January 19): Capricorn's strong focus on career and ambition may clash with Cancer's desire for a warm and nurturing home life. Cancer can feel neglected or second to Capricorn's professional goals.

4. Sagittarius (November 22 - December 21: Sagittarius's love for adventure and exploration may not align with Cancer's need for emotional closeness and

stability. Cancer might feel that Sagittarius is too free-spirited and commitment-averse.

5. Aquarius (January 20 - February 18): Aquarius values intellectual pursuits and independence, which can sometimes make them seem detached from emotional matters. Cancer may find it challenging to connect with Aquarius on a deep emotional level.

It's important to remember that astrology provides general insights, and individual compatibility can vary widely. While these signs may present challenges for Cancer, strong, healthy relationships can still be built with individuals from any zodiac sign through effective communication, compromise, and mutual understanding.

Who Gets on Best with Cancer:

―――

Cancer individuals are known for their nurturing and sensitive nature.

They tend to get along well with certain zodiac signs that complement their characteristics and values. Here are some zodiac signs that often form strong and harmonious connections with Cancer:

1. Taurus (April 20 - May 20): Taurus and Cancer share a deep appreciation for home and family life. They both value stability, comfort, and emotional security, making their bond strong and enduring.

2. Virgo (August 23 - September 22): Virgo's practical and caring nature aligns well with Cancer's nurturing tendencies. They both pay attention to detail and enjoy taking care of their loved ones.

3. Scorpio (October 23 - November 21): Scorpio and Cancer share intense emotional connections. They both understand the depths of emotions and are willing to explore the complexities of their feelings together.

4. Pisces (February 19 - March 20): Pisces is highly intuitive and compassionate, which resonates with Cancer's emotional depth. They create a safe and loving environment for each other, where they can express their feelings openly.

5. Capricorn (December 22 - January 19): Capricorn's stability and Cancer's nurturing qualities complement each other. Capricorn provides a sense of security, while Cancer offers emotional support and care.

6. Leo (July 23 - August 22): Despite their differences, Cancer and Leo can have a strong bond. Leo's confidence and Cancer's nurturing nature create a balance, and they appreciate each other's strengths.

7. Sagittarius (November 22 - December 21): Cancer's emotional depth can balance Sagittarius's adventurous spirit. They can help each other grow by exploring new experiences together.

Remember that astrology provides general insights, and individual compatibility depends on various factors, including personal values, communication, and shared interests. While these signs tend to get along well with Cancer, meaningful relationships can be formed with individuals from any zodiac sign through mutual understanding and effort.

What Are Cancer Individuals Into:

Cancer individuals are known for their unique interests and preferences. They are drawn to activities and hobbies that resonate with their nurturing and sensitive nature. Here are some of the things Cancer individuals are into:

1. Cooking and Baking: Cancer individuals often have a deep love for culinary arts. They enjoy preparing delicious meals and treats, especially for their loved ones. Cooking and baking provide a sense of comfort and satisfaction.

2. Home Decor: Cancerians have a strong attachment to their homes and take pride in creating warm and cozy living spaces. They are often interested in interior design and enjoy decorating their homes with a personal touch.

3. Gardening: Many Cancer individuals have a green thumb and find solace in gardening. Tending to plants and creating beautiful gardens is a way for them to connect with nature and find relaxation.

4. Art and Creative Expression: Cancerians often have a creative side and may enjoy art, crafting, or other forms of creative expression. They use these outlets to express their emotions and feelings.

5. Caring for Others: Nurturing is a core trait of Cancer individuals. They into activities that involve taking care of others, whether it's looking after family members, volunteering, or working in healthcare.

6. Collecting Memorabilia: Cancer individuals may have a penchant for collecting sentimental items and memorabilia. These items hold emotional significance and help them preserve memories.

7. Emotional Exploration: Cancerians are naturally introspective and may have an interest in psychology, self-help, and personal growth. They enjoy delving into their own emotions and understanding human behavior.

8. Beach Retreats: Many Cancer individuals have a deep connection to water, and they often find solace by the beach. Beach vacations and retreats by the sea are particularly appealing to them.

9. Vintage and Antique Finds: Cancerians may have an appreciation for vintage and antique items. They are drawn to the history and stories behind old objects.

10. Family Traditions: Cancer individuals cherish family traditions and may be into preserving and passing down customs, rituals, and family recipes.

It's important to remember that while these are common interests among Cancer individuals, personal preferences can vary. Cancerians may have a combination of these interests or unique hobbies that reflect their individuality.

The 12 zodiac signs compatibility

Cancer & Aries Love Compatibility:

A Rollercoaster of Emotions

Cancer And Aries Emotional Connection (70%)

Cancer and Aries make for an intriguing pair in the realm of emotional intimacy. Cancer, known for its nurturing and emotional depth, may initially view Aries as brash and emotionally distant. However, beneath Aries' fiery exterior lies a desire for meaningful connections and tenderness. This union has the potential to ignite a sensual and exciting sexual relationship that blooms when both partners find the right balance.

Cancer & Aries Trust Issues (50%)

Trust can be a touchy subject in the Cancer-Aries relationship. Fidelity is usually not a significant concern, but the trust issues often revolve around intimacy. Aries' straightforward and assertive approach may come across as pushy and inconsiderate to Cancer. Conversely, Cancer's emotional intensity might feel overwhelming to Aries. Mutual understanding and patience are key to building trust and easing these concerns.

Cancer & Aries Communication Challenges (20%)

Effective communication can be a challenge for Cancer and Aries due to their impulsive natures. Both are prone to cut conversations short before reaching the heart of the matter. While their cardinal qualities provide some common ground, their divergent interests often lead to distracted discussions. To overcome this, both partners must approach conversations thoughtfully and avoid rushing. It's essential to recognize that their differences can be a source of strength, rather than a hindrance.

Cancer & Aries Shared Values (40%)

Cancer values emotional stability and a rational approach, while Aries places importance on energy, focus, and consistency. Their value systems aren't inherently aligned, except for a shared belief in the potential benefits of achieving a balance in life. Finding common ground may require compromise and an understanding of each other's perspectives.

Cancer & Aries Shared Activities (30%)

Aries thrives on physical activities and creative pursuits, while Cancer prefers rest, indulgence, and emotional bonding. Their shared activities often center around sexual intimacy and downtime. Finding a balance between Aries' energetic pace and Cancer's desire for relaxation may pose a challenge.

In Summary (47%)

The Cancer-Aries relationship is not for the faint of heart; it demands effort and adaptability from both partners. While it can be a rocky road, the rewards include a profound understanding of passion, deep emotions, and the ability to create a truly unique connection. If they can overcome their differences and embrace their individual strengths, this union can lead to a fulfilling and passionate partnership that both partners may find unmatched elsewhere.

Cancer & Taurus

Love Compatibility: A Profound Connection

Cancer And Taurus Emotional Bond (95%)

Cancer and Taurus, often perceived as reserved signs, share a surprising and passionate connection. Both signs have a deep appreciation for physical pleasure, though they approach it differently. Taurus, guided by Venus, embraces sensuality and aims to satisfy their partner completely. Cancer, on the other hand, seeks emotional closeness and yearns for trust in their sexual relationship. Taurus' gentle touch and ability to relax Cancer can create a profound level of intimacy and trust. However, if neither partner possesses a strong sexual drive, they may find themselves in an asexual relationship, focusing on other aspects of life.

Cancer & Taurus Trust and Devotion (99%)

Trust is the foundation of the Cancer-Taurus relationship. These partners rely on their intuitive understanding and seldom face trust issues. Their shared goals of love, family, and a sense of home further cement their devotion to one another. Their connection runs so deep that betraying their trust would be a rare occurrence. For them, love, loyalty, and the comfort of home are paramount.

Cancer & Taurus Communication and Understanding (80%)

Cancer and Taurus share a strong emotional connection and communicate through subtle cues and shared interests. They are attuned to each other's unspoken words and prioritize topics like love, family, and children. However, Taurus can be exceptionally stubborn at times, shutting down conversations when their core beliefs are challenged. Cancer may find this frustrating, but with patience and gentleness, they can navigate such moments and ensure effective communication.

Cancer & Taurus Emotionally Deep (99%)

Taurus and Cancer are masters of the emotional realm. Both signs excel at expressing their emotions, albeit in distinct ways. Cancer uses its nurturing nature to care for its Taurus partner emotionally, while Taurus responds with physical tenderness, material security, and practicality—qualities cherished by Cancer. This emotional exchange between them creates a continuous chain reaction of love, deepening their bond. When obstacles arise, they muster the energy to fight for their love and protect their relationship.

Cancer & Taurus Shared Values (80%)

Cancer and Taurus share a deep appreciation for life and peace. Both value the qualities associated with the Moon, such as family, compassion, understanding, and happiness. However, there may be a slight divergence when it comes to material matters. Cancer leans toward the emotional value of life, while Taurus emphasizes financial security due to concerns about their material well-being. Nevertheless, if they have a family, their perspectives often shift, recognizing the true value of money in providing for their loved ones.

Cancer & Taurus Mutual Activities (90%)

Cancer and Taurus enjoy sharing a variety of activities, although their definition of "activity" may involve relaxation and indulgence. Both find pleasure in the simple acts of sleeping, eating, or simply doing nothing. Their shared downtime is an essential aspect of their relationship, strengthening their emotional bond.

In Summary (91%)

The union of Taurus and Cancer is marked by a profound and enduring connection. Their shared emotional goals—love, understanding, family, and the comfort of home—bind them closely. This relationship exudes a sense of perpetual love and emotional depth, with the potential to overcome any challenges that may arise. Despite individual emotional baggage, their shared love will likely lead them to the fulfilling and loving relationship they desire.

Cancer & Gemini

Love Compatibility: Bridging Differences

Cancer And Gemini Intimacy Connection (5%)

The sexual and intimate connection between Cancer and Gemini is challenging. Gemini's love for unconventional and adventurous experiences clashes with Cancer's desire for emotional intimacy. While there may be a strong link between them, it's rare for Gemini to draw Cancer into their sexual escapades. For this to work, Cancer must communicate their emotions openly, and Gemini must have the patience to discuss things repeatedly. A balanced approach is required for their sexual life to be mutually satisfying.

Cancer & Gemini Trust and Freedom (25%)

Trust can be a touchy issue for Cancer and Gemini. Gemini, ruled by Mercury, is prone to restlessness and values freedom. They may be hesitant to fully trust their Cancer partner if they feel their independence is at risk. Cancer's task in this relationship is to allow Gemini their freedom. When they live together, it can pose a challenge, with Gemini frequently spending time away. Trust remains intact as long as both partners prioritize their values and refrain from trivial lies.

Cancer & Gemini Communication and Understanding (70%)

Gemini's communication skills are well-known, and they can talk to almost anyone. They often feel the need to open up more with Cancer and share things they wouldn't with others. Cancer emits a nurturing aura that encourages

Gemini to express their inner child. This connection can lead to a long-lasting relationship characterized by deep emotional and sexual understanding.

Cancer & Gemini Emotional Dynamics (10%)

Gemini's tendency to avoid in-depth emotional conversations can frustrate Cancer, who desires emotional closeness. Cancer may be disappointed by Gemini's inability to recognize and respond to their emotions. While Cancer seeks emotional depth, Gemini's superficial approach to feelings may make them appear emotionally distant.

Cancer & Gemini Value Systems (1%)

Cancer and Gemini have fundamentally different value systems. Cancer places high value on emotions and heartfelt connections, while Gemini is more focused on rational thinking and mental stimulation. These differences can create conflict in their relationship, especially when it comes to what each partner values in life and love.

Cancer & Gemini Shared Activities (15%)

Shared activities between Cancer and Gemini depend on Cancer's energy level. If Cancer can keep up with Gemini's dynamic schedule, they can enjoy various experiences together, including travel. However, Gemini's insatiable curiosity and desire for new experiences may eventually clash with Cancer's preference for settling down and building a family. Gemini's freedom-loving nature doesn't align with Cancer's desire for stability.

In Summary (21%)

Gemini and Cancer are zodiac neighbors, often finding compatibility in friendship. However, when it comes to romantic and sexual relationships, significant differences emerge. For their relationship to thrive, both partners must make adjustments. Cancer must accept Gemini's need for freedom and adventure, while Gemini needs to be open to Cancer's emotional needs. If they can offer each other freedom and understanding, they have the potential to experience a love reminiscent of a child's first crush.

Cancer & Cancer

Cancer And Cancer Intimacy Connection (65%)

Cancer individuals are masters of emotional intimacy, and when two Cancer partners come together, they delve deep into each other's emotional cores through their sex life. Their approach may lack initiative, as Mars, the planet of action, falls in Cancer. To have a satisfying sex life, they must awaken their inner desires and be open to experimentation. While they may not be the most adventurous in bed, their physical connection is grounded in their deep emotions and love for each other.

Cancer & Cancer Trust and Stability (99%)

Trust is natural between two Cancer partners. Both value emotional stability and understand the imperfections of the human condition. They seek a loving, stable home and family, which creates a strong foundation for trust. Neither has the inclination to betray the other, as their goals align in love and the nurturing of their family.

Cancer & Cancer Communication and Connection (90%)

Communication between two Cancer partners is often non-verbal and deeply intuitive. They can spend days together in comfortable silence. While they share life details with each other, they cherish moments of quiet connection. Verbal communication may not be a priority for them, as their shared understanding transcends words. They communicate through shared glances, smiles, and unspoken emotions.

Cancer & Cancer Emotional Bond (99%)

Both Cancer individuals are deeply emotional, and their bond revolves around family and closeness. They are experts at understanding each other's emotional states. Their relationship often serves as a platform to resolve issues from their families of origin. As Moon-ruled signs, their mood changes often coincide, but their emotional depth goes beyond what meets the eye. They share their emotions, work through them together, and build a loving family life based on mutual understanding.

Cancer & Cancer Shared Values (99%)

In the realm of shared values, Cancer-Cancer partners align perfectly. They both cherish emotional clarity, peace, and the creation of a serene family life. These values provide a solid foundation for their relationship, allowing them to thrive even when they initially seem mismatched.

Cancer & Cancer Shared Activities (55%)

Cancer-Cancer pairs can engage in shared activities with ease, thanks to their similar interests and values. However, their passive natures may lead to stagnation over time. They can fall into a routine of comfort and familiarity, potentially missing out on new experiences. To maintain excitement in their relationship, they should make an effort to plan activities and maintain physical intimacy.

In Summary (85%)

Cancer-Cancer couples may need to overcome potential stagnation in their sex life and shared activities. Their relationship thrives on emotional depth and the shared values of family, peace, and clarity. However, they must keep their relationship fresh and vibrant to avoid monotony. Overall, their deep emotional connection makes them great candidates for a loving marriage and family life. If they address potential shortcomings and maintain their emotional harmony, their bond can remain strong.

Cancer & Leo

Cancer And Leo Intimacy Connection (30%)

Cancer and Leo are an intriguing couple, representing the two luminaries of the zodiac – the Moon and the Sun. They are often likened to a king and queen but, when it comes to sex, it's like a king and queen with little chemistry. Their sexual connection hinges on their deep emotions, but Leo's fiery and passionate approach can intimidate Cancer. Cancer seeks tenderness, while Leo's nature tends to be more forceful. Their sexual encounters can lack excitement, making compromise and understanding crucial.

Cancer & Leo Trust (50%)

Leo enjoys being the center of attention, and this need may test Cancer's trust. However, if Cancer feels truly loved, they won't doubt their partner based on their nature. Nevertheless, differences may lead both partners to secretly seek more compatible options. The key to trust here is mutual understanding and acceptance.

Cancer & Leo Communication And Intellect (10%)

Cancer and Leo, ruled by the Moon and the Sun, respectively, have contrasting perspectives and communication styles. Their conversations may lead them to drift apart as they often view things differently. Leo's need to shine and command attention can make Cancer feel overshadowed. Their ability to find common ground may come from addressing mysteries and issues that require a dual perspective. Respect for each other's unique qualities can help bridge their communication gaps.

Cancer & Leo Emotions (45%)

Cancer represents motherly love and family emotions, while Leo embodies joy, fun, and passion. Cancer seeks deep emotional connections, while Leo wants to express love exuberantly. This disparity may lead to misunderstandings as Leo wants to shout their love from the rooftops, which may seem inauthentic to Cancer. Opposing Saturn-ruled signs, they both have much to learn from their contrasting approaches.

Cancer & Leo Values (1%)

Cancer values tenderness, emotions, family, and stability, while Leo values initiative, passion, energy, and recognition. Their value systems rarely align, making it challenging for them to prioritize the same things.

Cancer & Leo Shared Activities (35%)

Leo's social nature may clash with Cancer's preference for intimate, quieter activities. Cancer enjoys time with close friends, walks by the lake, or romantic evenings, while Leo seeks social recognition and likes being seen. Finding common ground is challenging, as Leo wants to be the center of attention, something that Cancer doesn't naturally desire.

In Summary (29%)

Cancer and Leo are special individuals, strong in their own ways. Their mission in relationships often involves spreading love to less fortunate signs. They may not have a deep emotional connection due to their contrasting natures. Leo's fiery and passionate approach can intimidate Cancer, while Cancer's tender nature may not align with

Leo's exuberant expression of love. Trust may be tested, and communication may be challenging. However, their differences can be an opportunity for growth if they learn to appreciate each other's unique qualities. While their love may not be traditional, it can still serve a unique purpose in the world.

Cancer & Virgo

Cancer And Virgo Intimacy Connection (95%)

Cancer and Virgo have the potential for a lasting and inspiring love. Their sexual relationship is like a lecture on emotions. Virgo, ruled by Mercury, may initially struggle to connect with their emotions. They tend to analyze and overthink, making it difficult for them to feel and enjoy sex fully. Cancer, with their deep emotional connection, may have unrealistic expectations due to their difficulty in comprehending Virgo's emotional process. Over time, they can better understand each other's unique emotional needs, forming a stronger sexual bond.

Cancer & Virgo Trust (99%)

Cancer's stability and emotional commitment make them a trustworthy partner for Virgo. Cancer's choice to be with Virgo is a testament to their commitment. Both signs value a loving family and shared life, reducing doubts and insecurities in their relationship.

Cancer & Virgo Communication And Intellect (60%)

Cancer and Virgo face challenges in communication due to their contrasting emotional and rational natures. Virgo's analytical approach often conflicts with Cancer's emotional sensitivity. However, when their intellectual strengths and emotional understanding align, their communication becomes inspiring and magical. Accepting each other's differences is key to successful communication.

Cancer & Virgo Emotions (65%)

Virgo's rationality can dampen their overall emotional state, leading to an analysis of their feelings. Cancer may find this off-putting, as they value emotional expression. Understanding and patience are vital for a healthy emotional connection. Virgo's emotional side, often hidden, needs a trusting environment to thrive.

Cancer & Virgo Values (50%)

Cancer values family, love, and understanding, while Virgo values intellect, attention to detail, and health. Their differing values can pose challenges in their relationship, requiring compromise and acceptance to bridge the gap.

Cancer & Virgo Shared Activities (90%)

Cancer and Virgo do not necessarily need shared activities to thrive. Both signs can manage without each other, making them flexible in their choices. Their rational compatibility helps them make arrangements for their time together. While they may not prioritize shared activities, they can still enjoy doing things together, fostering a sense of togetherness.

In Summary (77%)

Cancer and Virgo can form a deep and lasting bond, often initiated by a strong sexual connection. While they may face challenges due to their differing emotional and rational approaches, their willingness to understand and accept each other's unique qualities can lead to a remarkable relationship. Their differences complement each other, making them an inspirational couple. With patience and open hearts, they can create a fulfilling and enduring love.

Cancer & Libra

Cancer And Libra Intimacy Compatibility (40%)

Cancer and Libra may appear distant at first, primarily due to their shared difficulty in embracing passion and initiative in their sexual life. While Libra's tactful and considerate nature can have a soothing effect on Cancer, their differing elemental attributes pose a challenge. Cancer is a Water sign, and Libra is an Air sign, leading to potential discrepancies in the speed and emotional depth of their connection. To improve their sex life, Cancer and Libra should aim to build a foundation of friendship and shared emotions.

Cancer & Libra Trust (30%)

Cancer values trust and seeks a quiet, family-oriented life. In contrast, Libra's need for constant social interaction and approval can create doubts in Cancer's mind. Cancer may question whether Libra is the right partner for a stable family life. On the other hand, Libra may find Cancer's approach to a romantic relationship unrealistic. Trust can become a significant issue in their relationship.

Cancer & Libra Communication And Intellect (50%)

As signs ruled by Venus and the Moon, Cancer and Libra place importance on their relationship. While their communication may not be overly challenging, they may not share many interests or have the necessary mutual respect for quality communication. Unrealistic plans can lead to conflicts. Cancer's practicality may clash with Libra's more idealistic approach, creating tensions.

Cancer & Libra Emotions (15%)

Both Cancer and Libra are highly emotional signs. However, their emotional contexts differ greatly. Cancer seeks earthly love and a grounded connection, while Libra desires a spiritual, balanced love. This disparity in emotional needs can result in a prolonged and unsatisfying relationship, with both partners waiting for a breakthrough that may never come.

Cancer & Libra Values (20%)

Cancer and Libra both value pleasant and joyful connections between people, but their system of values diverges significantly. While Cancer values tenderness and care, Libra values responsibility and platonic love. This fundamental difference in values poses a challenge to their compatibility.

Cancer & Libra Shared Activities (10%)

While Cancer and Libra can engage in various activities, their willingness to do so may be limited. Cancer's desire for a safe base combined with Libra's need for someone to challenge them can lead to frustration. Libra may not fulfill Cancer's desire to travel the world, and their differences can create tension in their shared activities.

In Summary (28%)

Cancer and Libra face significant challenges in their relationship, primarily due to differences in values, trust issues, and emotional needs. Their emotional and practical disparities can make it difficult for them to find common ground and create a harmonious connection. To make their relationship work, both partners must embrace their independence and focus on love while addressing their individual priorities. It may require compromises and understanding on both sides to build a lasting love.

Cancer & Scorpio

Cancer And Scorpio Intimacy Compatibility (90%)

Cancer and Scorpio are a passionate and deeply connected couple. Despite Scorpio's association with darker themes, Cancer understands and supports their Scorpio partner's need to express their deepest emotions and desires in their sex life. This intimate connection can be highly satisfying for both partners if Cancer does not feel forced or scared into doing something they are not ready for. Their shared emotional depth enhances their sexual experiences.

Cancer & Scorpio Trust (95%)

Trust is paramount for Scorpio when they fall in love. Betrayal can trigger Scorpio's possessive and jealous tendencies, and they can become suspicious. Cancer values trust and seeks a stable, secure family life, making them a trustworthy partner. Both signs can provide the security needed to build and maintain trust in the relationship.

Cancer & Scorpio Communication And Intellect (99%)

Cancer and Scorpio often understand each other without needing to verbalize their thoughts. Their communication is exceptionally strong, with the ability to finish each other's sentences. Their deep emotional connection allows them to talk about almost anything, making their mental connection extraordinary. When they share an emotional link, their communication is non-verbal and highly intuitive.

Cancer & Scorpio Emotions (70%)

Cancer lives deeply immersed in their emotions and integrates them into their everyday life. Scorpio, however, tends to repress emotions and focuses on reaching their goals. Finding a balance is crucial for both partners to ensure emotions flow naturally without impeding their objectives. They both need to learn to lose control, regain it, and allow emotions to ebb and flow freely.

Cancer & Scorpio Values (25%)

Cancer values inner peace and craves a stable family life. Scorpio, on the other hand, seeks change and is driven by a desire for transformation. While their values regarding relationships align, their fundamental values differ significantly. Both partners must be flexible and understand these differences to make the relationship work.

Cancer & Scorpio Shared Activities (95%)

Cancer and Scorpio are adaptable in their shared activities. They are devoted to protecting their loved ones and share a strong sense of responsibility. While Scorpio may prefer more daring activities, they can adjust to Cancer's milder preferences. Their shared activities are a testament to their deep connection and can involve a wide range of experiences.

In Summary (79%)

Cancer and Scorpio share a profound connection that allows them to understand each other on a profound level. They can explore love and intimacy in ways that are often unattainable for other zodiac signs. However, their relationship can become challenging if Scorpio suppresses their emotions or becomes insensitive. Maintaining emotional sincerity and purity is crucial for their intense connection to thrive, allowing them to deepen their love and understanding.

Cancer & Sagittarius

Cancer And Sagittarius Intimacy Compatibility (40%)

Cancer and Sagittarius are unlikely to be attracted to each other, and their sexual and intimate compatibility is often challenging. Sagittarius has a changeable nature that Cancer may struggle to understand due to their need for emotional security. For their sexual relationship to work, trust needs to be established, and genuine emotions must be shared. Sagittarius can bring a sense of fun and adventure to their sex life, but Cancer may find it challenging to let go of their preconceptions and insecurities.

Cancer & Sagittarius Trust (1%)

Trust can be a significant issue in a Cancer-Sagittarius relationship. Sagittarius's tendency to be flirtatious and seek the affection of many can trigger feelings of jealousy and mistrust in Cancer. Sagittarius may not fully grasp Cancer's need for emotional security, which can result in a lack of trust on both sides. This lack of trust can lead to conflicts and misunderstandings, potentially putting the relationship in jeopardy.

Cancer & Sagittarius Communication And Intellect (60%)

Both Cancer and Sagittarius share a love for knowledge, which can be a common ground for their communication. However, they may have different paces and styles of discussing topics. Sagittarius might find Cancer's communication slow, while Cancer might perceive Sagittarius as superficial or overly philosophical.

If they share a passion and choose the same profession, their communication can be enriched. They generally understand each other's thinking processes and can address various issues through open conversation.

Cancer & Sagittarius Emotions (10%)

Cancer and Sagittarius have contrasting emotional natures, as Cancer is a Water sign and Sagittarius is a Fire sign. They tend to experience love at different intensities, paces, and moments. Sagittarius falls in love passionately and swiftly, while Cancer takes time to build emotional security before expressing their feelings. This discrepancy can lead to misunderstandings and mismatches in their emotional connection.

To make their relationship work, Sagittarius needs to exhibit patience and respect Cancer's need for emotional stability. Cancer, in turn, must take a leap of faith and be open to the idea of love developing at a different pace than they are accustomed to.

Cancer & Sagittarius Values (45%)

Cancer and Sagittarius have different values, but they can appreciate certain aspects of each other. Cancer values Sagittarius' honesty and emotional spontaneity, while Sagittarius appreciates Cancer's dedication and compassion. Despite these differences, they share a common interest in acquiring knowledge, which can create a connection between them.

Cancer & Sagittarius Shared Activities (5%)

Finding shared activities that both Cancer and Sagittarius can enjoy is challenging. They have distinct approaches and paces when it comes to activities, making it difficult for them to engage in things together. Cancer may find Sagittarius's rapid pace and constant movement irritating, while Sagittarius could perceive Cancer as a hindrance to their desire for exploration.

In Summary (27%)

Cancer and Sagittarius are not typically attracted to each other, and their relationship is often marked by challenges. While they can have moments of connection, their differences in emotional intensity and values can create significant hurdles. To make the relationship work, both partners must be patient, open to compromise, and willing to appreciate each other's unique qualities. However, success in the long term is rare for this pairing, and strong support from their individual horoscopes is essential for them to sustain a lasting connection.

Cancer & Capricorn

Cancer And Capricorn Intimacy Compatibility (99%)

Cancer and Capricorn, despite being opposing signs, share a strong attraction and become perfect lovers for one another. The patience and emotional depth that Capricorn brings to the relationship is precisely what Cancer needs to feel secure and explore their sensual side. Capricorn, on the other hand, desires a partner who values true emotion and does not take sex lightly. Their sexual compatibility is highly satisfying, and Cancer's compassion and warmth complement Capricorn's lack of love and emotional expression.

Cancer & Capricorn Trust (99%)

Trust is a vital aspect of the Cancer-Capricorn relationship. Capricorn may appear to be a cautious and somewhat untrusting sign due to their concerns and meticulous approach to relationships. However, they understand that trust is essential to their partner, and they will demonstrate it. Cancer's moral values and sincerity create a trusting environment for Capricorn, allowing them to feel secure in the relationship.

Cancer & Capricorn Communication And Intellect (70%)

Cancer and Capricorn share a deep, unspoken connection due to their shared family-oriented approach and the resonance of their ancestors' values. Their communication is often characterized by a sense of familiarity and warmth, as if they have known each other for a long time. However, if this connection is not established immediately, Capricorn may come across as too career-focused and emotionally distant, while Cancer may seem overly clingy or housewifely. Both partners should recognize that their negative perceptions are likely projections of their inner opposite sides, preventing them from feeling complete.

Cancer & Capricorn Emotions (75%)

Cancer and Capricorn carry a karmic bond from their ancestors, and their emotional states are intertwined with their expectations from each other and their relationship. Despite their differences, both signs have the capacity for strong emotions. Capricorn's emotional depth can be challenging to reach, but Cancer is drawn to this challenge and considers it a life mission to connect with their partner on a profound level. They may experience intense emotional states when they meet. However, they should avoid trying to change each other, as acceptance is key to a successful and harmonious relationship.

Cancer & Capricorn Values (70%)

Cancer and Capricorn share a common value system, particularly regarding stability and practicality. Despite their opposing signs, they both cherish stability and security in their lives. They appreciate partners who provide a sense of reliability and safety, making this one of the core values they share.

Cancer & Capricorn Shared Activities (90%)

Finding shared activities that both Cancer and Capricorn enjoy is relatively easy. They are both flexible and open to adjusting their plans to accommodate each other's preferences. By respecting each other's boundaries and personal tastes, they can easily agree on various activities to engage in together. Their time spent together is likely to be highly satisfying as long as they maintain this level of mutual respect.

In Summary (84%)

Cancer and Capricorn are often destined to relive a love story that transcends time and generations. This relationship is deeply rooted in karmic bonds and the need to address unresolved emotions from their family history. To experience the full potential of their connection, they must first address these issues. Once they have cleared these emotional debts, they are likely to choose each other without hesitation. Their relationship can be a once-in-a-lifetime love that offers both partners a deep and meaningful connection.

Cancer & Aquarius

Cancer And Aquarius Intimacy Compatibility (1%)

A sexual relationship between Cancer and Aquarius can be challenging for both partners. Despite Cancer's sensitive nature, they can become rough and distant when setting strong boundaries, causing stress in their sexual interactions. Aquarius, although known for innovation, is a fixed sign and may struggle to change their ways. They have a need for physical grounding, which can be incompatible with Cancer's desire for emotional connection during sex. To find sexual harmony, both partners must compromise, experiment, and engage in emotional exchange.

Cancer & Aquarius Trust (35%)

Trust can be a complex issue in a Cancer-Aquarius relationship. Cancer is typically loyal and honest, but their fear of upsetting their partner or causing an aggressive reaction can lead to a lack of transparency. Aquarius' liberal and sometimes unpredictable nature may seem eccentric to Cancer, creating inner mistrust. While both partners value honesty, they may struggle to trust the path their relationship is heading.

Cancer & Aquarius Communication and Intellect (55%)

Cancer and Aquarius can collaborate well intellectually. Cancer's attention to detail and interpersonal relationships complements Aquarius's broader perspective. They can turn grand ideas into reality, especially when involving a large group of people. However, they may face challenges in understanding each other's communication styles. Aquarius' unique way of expressing themselves can be puzzling to Cancer, who prefers a more emotional and direct approach. To foster understanding, Aquarius must see their Cancer partner as unique and worthy of examination.

Cancer & Aquarius Emotions (50%)

Aquarius' unconventional nature can disrupt Cancer's need for a peaceful and stable environment, creating the most significant emotional challenge in their relationship. Cancer thrives on a cozy and homely atmosphere, while Aquarius brings unpredictability and stress. Their expressions of love are quite distinct, but if they have children, they can focus their emotional energy on family life, creating a unique, boundary-free childhood for their kids. While their love may be unconventional, it will be strong, and they may have a hard time letting go.

Cancer & Aquarius Values (10%)

Cancer and Aquarius have different values that may appear irreconcilable. Cancer values stability, intimacy, and family, while Aquarius values freedom, intellect, and technology. Their differences in values can create challenges in the relationship. However, if they focus on their shared love for knowledge and learning, they may bridge the gap between their distinct values.

Cancer & Aquarius Shared Activities (25%)

Finding common activities can be challenging for Cancer and Aquarius. Cancer enjoys homey and traditional pursuits, while Aquarius seeks adventure and new experiences. One activity that may unite them is travel, as both have a shared desire for exploration. If they can find a balance between home life and travel, they might discover a shared passion that can bring them closer.

In Summary (31%)

Cancer and Aquarius may not be the typical happy couple, and their relationship is often filled with challenges. Their intimacy can be stressful for Cancer, and their lack of emotional connection can create tension. However, if they manage to find a common ground and understand each other's uniqueness, they might open up new perspectives and experiences. Both partners share a desire to learn and travel, and if they can balance home life and exploration, they may find a path to success in their relationship. Silent moments together could be the first step toward understanding and harmony.

Cancer & Pisces

Cancer And Pisces Intimacy Compatibility (85%)

Cancer and Pisces are often drawn together by deep romantic love. Their sexual connection is primarily emotional. Cancer brings intimacy and meaning to their sex life, nurturing their partner and creating a safe and stable environment for a healthy sexual relationship. Pisces, ruled by Venus, adds creativity, inspiration, and sensuality, enriching their sex life. The emotional bond between them is the key, and they cherish and respect each other's sensitivity.

Cancer & Pisces Trust (70%)

Cancer's tendency to create intimacy and a loving home can sometimes be perceived as pressure by Pisces.

Pisces may struggle to understand the importance of traditional concepts like marriage, and this can create tension. However, their strong emotional connection allows them to be patient and build trust in each other.

Cancer & Pisces Communication And Intellect (85%)

Pisces and Cancer communicate well, although Pisces can sometimes be scattered in their thoughts. Cancer values clarity and practicality, while Pisces may focus on abstract ideas and emotions. Pisces can sweep Cancer off their feet if they learn to rely on feelings and take action. However, words alone won't sustain their relationship; deeds must follow.

Cancer & Pisces Emotions (99%)

Cancer's empathetic nature allows them to understand Pisces on a deep level. Pisces often have a hidden emotional note in their world, and Cancer feels rather than listens, making them a perfect match for Pisces. This understanding fosters tenderness and emotional intimacy, creating a fairytale-like relationship.

Cancer & Pisces Values (25%)

Cancer values a stable emotional environment and a cozy home, while Pisces seeks excitement, magic, and beauty in life. Pisces may idealize partners and circumstances, and they can become disillusioned when faced with routine. A balance must be struck between the desire for stability and the need for excitement.

Cancer & Pisces Shared Activities (70%)

Cancer and Pisces start their relationship with many shared activities and excitement. Pisces' inspirational and creative nature blends well with Cancer's strength, stability, and roots. However, Pisces may desire more activity than Cancer needs in the long run. Open communication is essential to address this issue and avoid unnecessary problems.

In Summary (72%)

Cancer and Pisces share a deep emotional connection, often experiencing love at first sight. Their main challenge lies in Pisces' changeable nature, which they may fear showing. They prioritize different types of love in their lives, with Pisces seeking passionate and sensual love alongside family love, while Cancer desires the security of a family nest. Balancing excitement and stability is key to their success, and when achieved, they can become one of the most wonderful couples in the zodiac, with Cancer providing inspiration and Pisces a sense of home.

Unveiling the Romantic Essence of Every Zodiac Sign

How romantic they are

Aries - The Adventurous Romantic: Aries, represented by the fearless Ram, is known for their determination, strength, and bold energy. Their approach to love mirrors their impulsive nature as they fearlessly dive into challenging situations. In relationships, Aries individuals remain true to themselves and do not accommodate easily, making them moderate romantics who crave excitement.

Taurus - The Stable Romantic: Symbolized by the steadfast Bull, Taurus is an Earth sign seeking stability and comfort in love. Their loyalty and commitment attract partners, creating enduring romances. Taurus natives thrive in serene settings, surrounded by music, delightful food, and comforting scents, making them ideal for long-lasting love.

Gemini - The Cynical Romantic: Gemini, represented by the celestial twins, is an airy sign in perpetual pursuit of new experiences. While they bring a sense of variety and curiosity to relationships, their dual personalities can make them indecisive and emotionally vulnerable at times. To unlock their full romantic potential, Geminis need compatible partners.

Cancer - The Incredibly Romantic: As a water sign symbolized by the Crab, Cancer deftly transitions between emotional and materialistic aspects. Nurturers at heart, Cancer individuals understand their partners' desires and provide unwavering support, patience, and unconditional love. They embody the essence of a true romantic.

Leo - The Authentic Romantic: Leo, a fiery sign represented by the Lion, exudes vivacity, passion, and regal charisma. Their chivalry and passion attract admirers, but Leo's need for independence may pose challenges for some. They celebrate themselves and the idea of being in love, making them charismatic romantics.

Virgo - The Perfectionist in Romance: Virgo, symbolized by the Virgin, embodies purity and practicality. Their systematic approach to life extends to love, making them attentive listeners and loyal partners. They give their all in love and offer a refreshingly detailed perspective, making them perfect romantics.

Libra - The Demanding Romantic: Represented by the scales, Libra seeks balance in life. Their sociable nature and desire for reciprocity in love make them excellent romantics. They care for everyone and their partnerships, demanding symmetry in their relationships.

Scorpio - The Passionately Romantic: Scorpio, symbolized by the Scorpion, is a complex sign with fiery and watery traits. They struggle with trust issues but harbor intense emotions. Scorpios offer unparalleled passion and sensuality in love, creating deep connections with their partners.

Sagittarius - The Classic Unoriginal Romantic: Sagittarius, represented by the Archer, is known for its energy and pursuit of knowledge. They protect their partners and prioritize safety. While they may struggle to express themselves, they excel at understanding their partner's needs, adding a classic touch to romance.

Capricorn - The Realistic and Sincere Romantic: The last earthy sign, Capricorn, symbolized by the Goat, values tradition and seeks perfection in love. They are honest, responsible, and loyal partners, creating powerful romantic connections. They aim for confidence and power in their relationships.

Aquarius - The Carefree Romantic: Despite its name, Aquarius, an airy sign, focuses on humanitarianism and personal growth. Their carefree approach to romance values honesty and independence. They may not be traditional romantics but appreciate honesty in relationships.

Pisces - The Hopeless Romantic: The last sign of the zodiac, Pisces, a water sign with two fish, embodies compassion and love. They believe in fairy-tale romance, openly sharing their feelings with partners. Pisces individuals are dedicated and embrace the concept of "happily ever after." Zodiac Sign | Type of Attraction | Attraction Skills

Zodiac Sign	Type of Attraction	Attraction Skills
Aries	Adventurous romantic	4
Taurus	Stable romantic	5
Gemini	Cynical romantic	3
Cancer	Incredibly Romantic	5
Leo	Authentic romantic	4
Virgo	Perfectionist in romance	4

Libra | Demanding Romantic | 4

Scorpio | Passionately Romantic | 3

Sagittarius | Classic Unoriginal Romantic | 4

Capricorn | Realistic and Sincere Romantic | 4

Aquarius | Carefree Romantic | 3

Pisces | Hopeless Romantic | 5

IDEAL DATING PLACES

for Your Partner's Zodiac Sign

Expressing your love and appreciation for your partner is essential, especially in a fast-paced world where success and achievements often take center stage. Whether you've just met, have been dating for a while, or are in a long-term relationship or marriage, your partner will always cherish an expression of your genuine emotions. Having a partner by your side reminds you of your humanity, and it's equally important to make them feel valued in your life.

One of the best ways to show your partner that they hold a special place in your heart is by taking them out on a date. There are 12 zodiac signs, each with unique personality traits that influence their romantic preferences. Some share common traits, while others are entirely distinct from one another.

In this article, we will explore ideal dating places for each zodiac sign. If you're uncertain about your Ascendant zodiac sign, Indastro can help you determine it, enabling you to discover the perfect dating spots that align with your personality and make a great first impression, especially if it's your first date!

Aries, Scorpio, Sagittarius, and Pisces

These zodiac signs (ascendants) are highly romantic and enjoy open spaces. They have a natural inclination toward engaging in activities, making a picnic in a beautiful park or dining at open terrace restaurants surrounded by lush greenery an ideal date for them.

As adrenaline junkies, they are drawn to sports that align with their partner's interests, such as trekking and water rafting. Engaging in such activities keeps them on the edge of their seats and fills them with elation. A romantic beach stroll is a top choice for these signs, offering both romance and relaxation.

They also have a penchant for nightlife, making a night club or a late-night movie a frequent choice for their dates.

Taurus, Gemini, Virgo, and Libra

For these ascendants, emotional connection holds more significance than the venue itself. They value the genuine emotions, loyalty, and dedication of their partner over extravagant settings. An ideal date for them involves being in the company of someone with whom they can freely and openly communicate, without the need for extensive planning.

These individuals are highly adaptable, and any location chosen by their partner is perfect for them. If asked to make a choice, they often prefer quiet and peaceful places for their dates, where they can comfortably relax with their lover and engage in uninterrupted conversations. They have an affinity for various types of flowers, appreciating their different fragrances and colors.

While they may harbor deep feelings for someone, expressing those emotions can be a challenge. It takes time for them to muster the courage to share their love openly.

Cancer, Leo, Capricorn, and Aquarius

Long drives and trips epitomize the ideal dates for these ascendants. They are a highly dynamic bunch and dislike staying in one place, even during a date. They are deeply enamored with motion, making a long drive or a short trip to a distant location their idea of a great date. These individuals are enthusiastic about nightlife and enjoy vibrant and loud music, so don't be surprised if they invite you to a nightclub or a concert.

These ideal dating places cater to the unique personality traits of each zodiac sign, ensuring a memorable and enjoyable experience for both you and your partner. Whether you're exploring open spaces, seeking emotional connection, or embarking on exciting adventures, understanding your partner's zodiac sign can enhance your dating experiences and strengthen your bond.

Conclusion:

————

In this comprehensive guide, we've delved deep into the world of Cancer, one of the most intriguing and emotionally rich signs of the Zodiac. Throughout the chapters, we've explored the traits, characteristics, and quirks that make Cancer individuals truly unique. But our journey doesn't end here.

As we wrap up this book, we want to remind you that the horoscope for 2024, the likes and dislikes of a Cancer person, and much more await you in the pages that follow. Your exploration of the Cancer Zodiac sign has only just begun, and with the knowledge you've gained, you'll be better equipped to understand and connect with the Cancer individuals in your life.

So, whether you're a Cancer yourself or you're fascinated by the enigmatic world of this Water sign, dive into the horoscope, uncover the intricacies of a Cancer's preferences, and embrace the deep emotions that define this remarkable sign. The stars have much in store for those born under the sign of Cancer in 2024, and we're here to guide you through it all.

Thank you for embarking on this astrological journey with us. May the insights within these pages bring you clarity, understanding, and a deeper appreciation for the magic of Cancer.

Contact Us Thank You, Dear Reader

———

W e extend our sincere thanks to you, dear readers, for embarking on this astrological journey with us. Your curiosity, engagement, and trust have made this exploration of the Zodiac sign Cancer all the more fulfilling.

In these pages, we have delved into the essence of the Cancer sign, unveiling its secrets, traits, and the horoscope for 2024. We've ventured through the depths of emotion, explored the intricacies of relationships, and discovered the likes and dislikes of a Cancer individual. All of this would not have been possible without your interest and presence.

Your quest for knowledge and self-discovery is what fuels our passion for astrology, and we are grateful to have been your guides in this cosmic voyage. We hope that the insights and wisdom shared in these pages serve as a guiding light in your life.

We invite you to explore our other books, each dedicated to a unique Zodiac sign and various aspects of astrology. Whether you seek to deepen your understanding of the stars or uncover the mysteries of other signs, you'll find a wealth of knowledge waiting for you.

Should you have any questions, insights, or simply wish to connect with us, please don't hesitate to reach out.

You can contact us via **WhatsApp at +1 829-205-5456 or email us at danielsanjurjo47@gmail.com.**

May the stars continue to shine brightly on your path, and may your journey through the Zodiac signs be filled with enlightenment, growth, and harmony. **Sincerely Daniel Sanjurjo**

Did you love Cancer Zodiac Sign 2024? Then you should read The Dreams Interpretation Book[1] by Daniel Sanjurjo!

2

☐ Unlock the Secrets of Dreams with "Dreamscape Chronicles: A Journey into the World of Dreams"

☐ Are you ready to embark on a profound dream interpretation journey that will unveil the hidden meanings of your dreams, offering insights into your inner self, personal growth, and self-discovery? "Dreamscape Chronicles" is your definitive guide to navigating the enigmatic landscapes of the subconscious mind.

☐ Explore the Depths of Dream Analysis: Delve into the intricate world of dream interpretation, where the symbols and stories of the night come alive. From common dreams to the mysteries of the mind, this book unravels the symbolism and significance of your dreamscapes.

☐ Illuminate Your Path: Discover how dreams can inspire your creativity, provide therapeutic insights, and awaken your inner desires. This book serves as your compass, guiding you through the rich tapestry of dreams and helping you harness their potential.

☐ Key Topics Explored: Uncover the significance of dream symbolism, the role of common dream themes, and the influence of pioneers like Sigmund

Freud in understanding the profound landscapes of the dreamer's mind.

Are you ready to embark on a journey through the dreamer's world? "Dreamscape Chronicles" is your passport to the boundless landscapes of your own mind. Explore, interpret, and awaken to the possibilities hidden within your dreams.

Unlock the mysteries of your dreams and start your journey of self-discovery today!

Also by Daniel Sanjurjo

Zodiaco

Piscis 2024: Un Viaje Celestial

Zodiac world

Aries Revealed 2024

Taurus 2024 Leo 2024

Gemini 2024

Cancer Zodiac Sign 2024

Virgo 2024

Scorpio 2024

Sagittarius 2024 Horoscope

Capricorn Unveiled: A Cosmic Guide to 2024

Aquarius Horoscope 2024

Standalone

The Dreams Interpretation Book

About the Author

Daniel Sanjurjo is a passionate author who delves into the realms of astrology and self-help. With a gift for exploring the celestial and the human psyche, Daniel's books are celestial journeys of self-discovery and personal growth. Join the cosmic odyssey with this insightful writer.

Printed in Great Britain
by Amazon

34238648R00126